The World of Music

MAKING FRIENDS WITH MUSIC

PRELUDE

By

WILLIAM C. HARTSHORN

Supervisor of Music, Public Schools, Los Angeles, California; Instructor in Music Education, The University of Southern California

and

HELEN S. LEAVITT

Director of Music, Wheelock College, Boston, Massachusetts
Instructor in Music Appreciation, Boston University

I

GINN AND COMPANY

BOSTON · NEWYORK · CHICAGO · LONDON · ATLANTA · DALLAS · COLUMBUS · SAN FRANCISCO

351.9

ACKNOWLEDGMENTS

The authors wish to thank the group of educators and musicians who, either through research or by constructive suggestions, have contributed to the musical value of this book.

Acknowledgment is due for the use of themes from the following compositions:

Sir Edward Elgar's "Pomp and Circumstance No. 4," reproduced by special permission of the copyright owners, Boosey & Hawkes Ltd. and their agent, Boosey Hawkes Belwin, Inc.

London Suite by Eric Coates, used by permission of the composer and of the publishers, Chappell & Co., Ltd., London.

"Procession of the Sardar" and "In the Village" by M. Ippolitov-Ivanov and "Marguerite, Album Leaf" by Sergei Rachmaninov, used by permission of the publisher, Carl Fischer, Inc.

Der Rosenkavalier, by Richard Strauss, reprinted by permission; copyright 1911 and 1938 by Fürstner Ltd., London; sole agents for U. S. A., Galaxy Music Corporation, New York.

"Fugato on a Well-Known Theme," used by permission of the composer, Robert McBride.

Acknowledgment is also due for permission to use the poem "Romany Gold" from *Hearts Awake* by Amelia Josephine Burr, copyright 1919 by Doubleday, Doran & Company, Inc.

The authors wish to express their appreciation to Mr. Vahe Aslanian for providing the historical background and the words and music of "Zeitun March," and to Christine Turner Curtis for translations of the poems in A SONG PROGRAM; also to the Board of Education of Los Angeles for the photograph on the inside cover page.

FOREWORD

HAVE you ever stopped to think how much music there is in the world?

From the beginning nature has given us her share of it with bird songs, the noise of insects, the whistling or sighing of the wind, the regular beating or "swish" of the waves, the numberless other sounds which we can hear in the great out-of-doors. For many years also man has composed music, has cultivated a beautiful singing voice, and has developed musical instruments to produce unusual artistic effects beyond the power of the human voice.

Now modern invention has stepped into the picture and made it possible for us to hear all kinds of music any time and anywhere. Not so long ago, people who wished to hear music of one kind or another had to go to public auditoriums where the music would be presented. This meant buying tickets far ahead. It also meant that only a limited number of people could hear these concert programs, for the size of the audience depended upon the size of the auditorium and the price of the tickets.

Today tickets still are sold some weeks in advance for operas, for symphony concerts, or for recitals by well-known artists. But these and many other musical programs now may be heard by almost everyone in all parts of the world.

For the nineteenth century with its inventions has brought us new privileges, and you and I, by the turn of a dial, can bring all kinds of programs right into our homes or even into our automobiles. Distance makes little difference, and music played in California can be heard in Massachusetts as easily as though the two states were next door to each other.

Music of all kinds, from the latest song hits to grand opera, from popular dance music to the symphony, is ours if we care to listen. We can hear catchy tunes and rhythms that simply make us "keep time," whether we intend to or not.

We may not realize it, but in listening to all these numerous kinds of music we are gaining some ability in discovering different things which make certain compositions more pleasing than others. For example, one of the popular orchestras or bands plays a piece of music that we like, and all of a sudden we find ourselves moving either hands or feet, or both. No one has to tell us whether the music swings in twos or threes. We can feel it without being told. We can recognize the *rhythm*, even though we may not know the definition for it.

Or maybe we go to the movies, and the next thing we know we are whistling or humming some of the tunes which we heard as we watched the picture. So we find that we can recognize *melodies* as well as rhythm ; and these are two very important things in music.

Once in a while we hear a familiar tune, but there seems to be something strange about it. In this case, it may be the combination of sounds — the *harmony* — that attracts our notice. It is as though some friend appeared all dressed up in different and rather unusual clothes. The style of dress makes quite a change in his appearance, and we probably exclaim, "Why, I didn't recognize you at first."

This is because composers take tunes which we have heard over and over again and dress them up with new chords and harmonies, and sometimes the music sounds much better than it did in the first place. Sometimes it doesn't. At any rate, our ears let us know that these changes have been made, and so we develop the ability to recognize different effects in *harmony*.

This all amounts to one thing. We really know much more about music than we think we do. So it is a very easy matter to use the knowledge which has come to us naturally through hearing a great deal of music and apply it to the different compositions which are presented on the following pages.

CONTENTS

MAKING FRIENDS WITH MUSIC

PRELUDE

A COURSE FOR THE DEVELOPMENT

OF

MUSIC APPRECIATION

1

PARADE MUSIC EAST AND WEST

When you go to the movies do you pay much attention to the music? Do you remember the special phrase of music that introduces the news reel? Have you ever seen people make some motion in time to the music?

Almost everyone who is asked a question such as "How do you listen to music?" will answer, "With my ears." But there is more to it than just hearing.

In a motion picture or an opera the music is closely connected with the action on the screen or stage. So in listening to such music we must use our eyes as well as our ears. To carry this point one step further, many people, when they listen to someone playing the piano or some other instrument, like to sit near enough so that they can watch the action of the hands of the person who is playing.

Dr. Sigmund Spaeth (spāth), in his book *The Common Sense of Music*, says that a large number of persons "listen with their feet." He means that the accents in the music are so plain that there is a natural desire to "keep time" with them by some motion of the body. Because the rhythm arouses this desire for physical action, the music seems to be more interesting and attractive.

RHYTHM

Quite likely at some time or other each one of us has listened to music which has suggested something we might do. We have heard music to which we could skip, run, march, sway, or even make up dance steps.

Although "I've got rhythm" may be looked upon as a slang expression, still it is true of almost everybody. Rhythm is in nearly everything. If the heart does not beat in its proper rhythm we see a doctor. Day follows night in rhythmic order.

Success in sports is often due to the rhythmic action of the athlete. Slow-motion pictures show us the high degree of rhythm developed by a tennis player, a track star, or a diver, or reveal the rhythmic timing of the backfield shift (movements of the players) of a football team.

History tells us that rhythm came before melody (or tune, as some people call it), and the dance before the song. It is interesting to read how people who lived in very early times hollowed out logs or fastened pieces of wood together and covered them with skins. In beating upon these homemade instruments they discovered that the beats had various effects on the feelings of the people, as well as on their actions, and that even a sound of rhythmic beats produced a sense of pleasure.

Probably one reason why we enjoy watching a parade is that we like to hear the rhythmic music of the bands. When they come within hearing distance we begin to keep time to their music in some visible way, and even hum or whistle the tune if it is familiar or easy to catch. When a composer joins a lively rhythm with a pleasing melody and interesting harmony, his music is likely to remain popular for a long time, for people seldom tire of such a combination.

Pomp and Circumstance No. 4 [V. R. G 525 B

SIR EDWARD ELGAR (1857–1934), English composer. *Living in America at the same time:* KATHARINE LEE BATES.

Under the title of *Pomp and Circumstance* Sir Edward Elgar (ĕl′gär) wrote a set of six military marches. Only four of them have become generally known. They are all very dignified and suggest the idea of a royal procession, with all the military show that people like to see in times of peace.

It is said that the composer received the idea of the title *Pomp and Circumstance* from an English play by William Shakespeare (shāk′spēr), called *Othello* (ō-thĕl′ō). In Act III the hero, Othello, makes a farewell speech which closes with these words:

Farewell the neighing steed and the shrill trump,
The spirit-stirring drum, the ear-piercing fife,
The royal banner; and all quality,
Pride, pomp, and circumstance of glorious war.

When we repeat paragraphs from plays or verses from poems we often find words which are unusual and not in our vocabulary. So it may be necessary to look up the meaning of some of the words in these lines from *Othello* in order to understand just what Shakespeare meant.

The first in this set of six military marches is familiar to everyone. When the composer was asked to write an ode (a short poem suited to be set to music) for the crowning of King Edward VII of England, he used the trio, or middle section, of this march for the final chorus. It is an arrangement for voices and orchestra, with words written especially for the occasion by Arthur Christopher Benson. "Land of Hope and Glory" is the title of the chorus, and since the time of the royal ceremony it has been widely sung both in England and abroad.

"Pomp and Circumstance No. 4" is similar to the popular "No. 1" in the strength of its melodies and its brilliant parade of instruments. It was the last of the four marches to be given a public performance, and the other marches, "No. 5" and "No. 6," are still unknown.

As a motto for this set of marches Sir Edward Elgar has put on his original copy (this is commonly called the *score*) some lines by Lord de Talby, an English author:

> I hear the nation march
> Beneath her ensign as an eagle's wing;
> Moving to victory with solemn noise,
> With worship and with conquest
> And the voice of myriads.

THE MUSIC

This march is written for full orchestra. Although everyone knows what an orchestra is, the term *full orchestra* is used when the group of players is complete and all the instruments belonging to each of the sections, strings, woodwind, brass, and percussion, are present. A description of the instruments of the orchestra is given on page 141. It seems as though the composer enjoyed making even a military march an important composition, for he used all the instruments to express the show, eagerness, and life which belong to a military parade.

He also pointed out the way in which he wished his music to be played, for on the score*[1] we find certain terms of expression. Among these are *allegro marziale* (äl-lā′grō mär-tsĭ-ä′lā). *Allegro* means "quick, lively, and cheerful," and *marziale* means "martial," or "in the style of a march." *F* is an abbreviation for *forte* (fôr′tā), meaning "strong and firm." *Nobilmente* (nō-bĭl-mĕn′tā) means "nobly," or "in a grand manner," and *p* is an abbreviation for *piano* (pē-ä′nō), meaning "soft."

The two principal melodies are easy to follow.

FIRST MELODY

[1] As you read about the different musical compositions which are included in this book you will probably come across some words which are unfamiliar. These words are marked with a star (*) and on pages 135–144 they are defined and explained. Therefore if at any time there is doubt in your mind as to the exact meaning of a word, you will find it helpful to look it up. The correct idea as to what these musical words and terms mean will not only increase your understanding, but will add very much to your enjoyment of the music.

SECOND MELODY

This second melody occurs on page 142 of *Adventure* of THE WORLD OF MUSIC, and the instrumental background in the form of a piano accompaniment also is given with it.

HOW THIS COMPOSITION IS BUILT

Music, like a house, is divided into units. In a house these units are called *rooms*; in music they are called *sections*, or *divisions*. Just as each room has its own special furniture, so in music each section has its own special melody. In this way it is easy to discover a new section by a change in the melody, or, as it is usually called, the *theme*. The word *theme* means a musical idea or subject.

Another thing which helps us to recognize the way in which composers build their music is a sense of the rhythm. In our reading we have different marks of punctuation, such as the comma and period. In music the measures are grouped together in a rhythmic pattern called a *phrase*, and through the rhythm we can feel the ending of these phrases just as clearly as though there were a comma or a period.

In the first section of this music, "Pomp and Circumstance No. 4," the first two measures of the first melody are very important. They may be compared to a "musical motto"*; and they move about from one pitch to another, now up, now down. As the music moves along, it is easy to hear many different effects. The music is loud, then soft; it is in the major* mode* and changes to the minor* mode. Various instruments also seem especially important in certain places.

In the second section, when the strings play the smooth and stately melody, the entire mood of the composition seems to change from a joyful celebration to something more thoughtful and earnest. The music grows in power; the atmosphere becomes more exciting as the brass instruments repeat the melody and are supported by the full orchestra. It is as though a royal procession were passing before us with slow and stately steps.

A return of the first section brings still more changes, for both the rhythm and the harmony are brighter and more colorful. Then the second melody is heard once more. *Grandioso* (grän-dĭ-ō′sō), meaning "grand" or "noble," is marked on the score, and surely there is something splendid and regal about the performance.

In order that the principal theme, or first melody, shall not be forgotten in our eagerness for the second melody, the composer closes this march with a *coda,* in which parts of the first melody occur. Many times, after finishing a composition, the musician adds a few measures which, although not absolutely necessary, complete and strengthen the ending. These measures make up the section which is called the *coda.*

THE COMPOSER

A small English boy swinging his feet from a hard church pew and staring at the carvings of little animals and men in Worcester Cathedral — this is our first glimpse of the composer, Edward Elgar. Even as a child he would become excited at the sight or sound of anything beautiful.

Besides owning a music shop, his father was also a piano-tuner and an organist, so Elgar had a great deal of experience with music from his boyhood. No wonder that he became an organist, a leader of orchestras, and a composer.

Some of the qualities to be found in his music are an unaffected beauty and honesty, for Elgar was very humble about his musical ability. He always felt that what he had done was very small compared to the compositions written by the great masters who came before him. But his own music shows his originality and fine feeling in the expression of his love for beauty.

THINGS TO CONSIDER

1. Quite likely you have seen many parades and heard many marches.

   How does the music of "Pomp and Circumstance No. 4" compare with some compositions which you have heard before?

2. Examine the first and second melodies and check, in the following list, some words which may apply to each of them:

lively	joyful	grand	grave
splendid	steady	tender	rather slow
quiet	regal	merry	gay

3. There are marches written for parades and processions. There are marches written for concert programs.

   Would "Pomp and Circumstance No. 4" be more effective for one of these events than for the other?

   How?

4. One writer has said that this march presents in sound the color, sparkle, and romance of old military parades, when the prancing horses, flying banners, busbies (busbies are tall fur hats worn by some British soldiers: see the picture opposite page 74), and gay-colored uniforms brightened the procession of pomp and pageantry through London streets.

Do you agree?

5. It may help you in answering this question if you know that the two words *pomp* and *pageantry* mean about the same thing: a march or parade, which is more like a show or celebration when everything is bright and full of happiness.

Do you think that the composer has suggested such a merry affair or that he merely has expressed his feelings about it?
Has the composer used any one musical feature, such as rhythm, melody, or harmony, more than another?
If so, what is it?

6. Let us suppose that you are asked to write your opinion about this music, mentioning some of its chief qualities which appeal to you especially.

What can you say about it?

Procession of the Sardar [V. R. 11883 A

MICHAEL IPPOLITOV-IVANOV (1859–1935), Russian composer. *Living in America at the same time:* CHARLES EVANS HUGHES.

Have you ever read the story of Jason and the Golden Fleece?

If so, you will remember that the Golden Fleece was a valuable treasure which hung from a branch of a giant oak tree in Colchis (kōl′kĭs) Strand. Colchis Strand is not a name which someone has made up; it is a real place located on the eastern shore of the Black Sea. It is in Caucasia (kô-kā′shȧ), and Caucasia is a region between the Black Sea and the Caspian Sea.

Not far from Colchis Strand is a land of high mountains, plateaus, glaciers, and deep forests, called Georgia. It is one of the sections, or provinces, of Caucasia, and is right in the middle of the Caucasus (kô′kȧ-sŭs) Mountains in southeastern Europe.

Into this land have come peoples of many races and civilizations, for it is a natural bridge between Europe and Asia. Until the last part of the nineteenth century the people had no contact with modern civilization. Then oil was discovered, and the changes which resulted in the lives of the different peoples of that region were very great and came very rapidly. Shepherds learned to drill oil wells. Horsemen became miners, for in the mountains there are quantities of minerals which are valuable in industry.

Although the very simple, rustic nature of the country has largely disappeared, the Oriental traits still remain noticeable in the inhabitants, who have descended from the Slavs and belong to the Slavic race. (*Oriental* is a word used to describe countries in the East.)

THE SUITE

It was while he was living amid the colorful scenes of this Caucasian country that the composer Ippolitov-Ivanov (ēp-pō-lē′tôf ē′vän-ôf) composed a set of pieces called *Caucasian Sketches*. These *Caucasian Sketches* contain four musical tone pictures which are grouped together in a *suite** (swēt) to be played by a symphony orchestra.* Every suite is divided into parts, and when we consider the suite as one large composition we call these different parts *movements*. We may compare them to chapters in a story, for while they have some connection with each other, nevertheless each of them deals with a separate event.

In the *Caucasian Sketches* the fourth movement of the suite is called "Procession of the Sardar" (sär′där), although sometimes it has the title "March of the Caucasian Chief." But whether procession or march, its rhythm is most outstanding. The composition pictures the return of the victorious tribes headed by their chief, the Sardar. In this sketch Ippolitov-Ivanov has used a folk tune which has an interesting story behind it.

THE STORY

In what was once the state of Cilicia (sĭ-lĭsh′ĭ-ȧ), in years past situated in the middle of Armenia, there was a city called Zeitun (zȧ-tōōn′). It was located on the side of one of the Taurus (tô′rŭs) Mountains. The people who lived in this city were strong and brave, just as might be expected of people who live in the mountains, but they were very poor. Their principal occupation was farming and mining, and they raised wheat, grain, grapes, and olives. In Armenian the word *zeitun* means "olive," and the city received its name from the olive groves which were abundant in that land.

The people of Zeitun wanted their liberty, and several times they rebelled against the Turks who ruled them and were their bitter enemies. During one of these revolutions an Armenian composer named Choohajian (chōō-hä′jhän) wrote a patriotic song for the people of Zeitun to sing while they marched into battle. The words were written by a famous Armenian poet.

Zeitun March

We have lain quiet enough, brothers;
Let us surround them left and right.
Many enslaved people have become free;
Should we only remain humble and yielding?

Hail, Zeitun! Long live Zeitun!
May it not see slavery
While it has us as its sons.
Long live Zeitun! Hail, Zeitun!

Here is the music just as the people of Zeitun sang it.

Song of the People of Zeitun

The people liked the song so much that everybody sang it, and soon it spread all over the country, even to the Caucasian Mountains. Thus it seems probable that Ippolitov-Ivanov heard the song during his travels in the mountains, for he used its melody as the principal theme in the "Procession of the Sardar."

THE MUSIC

The beating of drums as though in the distance and the sound of triangle and cymbals in the introduction fix the march rhythm beyond a doubt. The first melody is heard softly at first, but it becomes stronger and louder as the different instruments enter.

Galloway

A Typical Scene in a Caucasian Village

B. P. Kudoyaroff

Caucasian Shepherds with Their Musical Instruments

Norwegian Travel Information Office

Grieg's Pine-wood Cabin (Exterior)

Knudsen

His Workroom (Interior)

FIRST MELODY

Piccolo and bassoon (three octaves apart)

This is followed by a new and different melody, which seems to remind us a little more of the East. The melody resembles a conversation. The first phrase* is played by the clarinet and bassoon.

SECOND MELODY (FIRST PHRASE)

This is answered by the oboe, with strings added later.

SECOND MELODY (SECOND PHRASE)

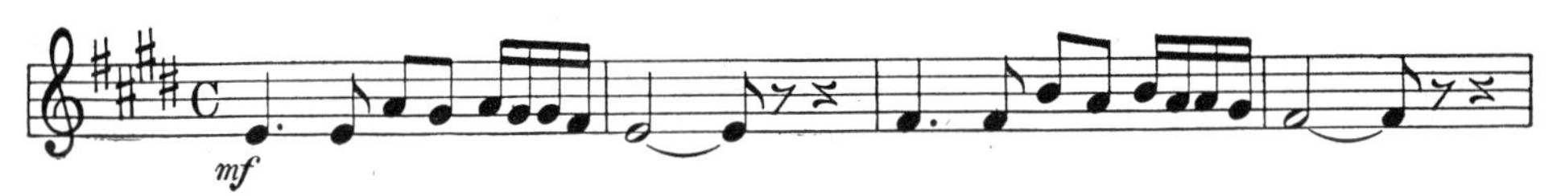

As the music moves along, it becomes more brilliant and alive; until we hear once more the first melody, played more slowly and with greater dignity. This makes us think of the pomp and splendor which suit the stately progress of the tribal leader, or chieftain. All the instruments join in this passage. This time the melody is followed by a codetta (kō-dĕt′tä) (which means "a short coda"), in which this rhythmic pattern stands out very clearly:

THINGS TO CONSIDER

1. Almost every piece of music has some features which are especially attractive and interesting. This composition is like all others in this respect, though of course it will not make the same appeal to everyone. If you were to listen to the record without knowing the title, do you think you could find some suggestion in the music as to:

a. The kind of occasion when it might be used?

b. The part of the world with which you can connect it?

c. Some picture or event which comes to your mind as you hear the music?

2. After learning the title and reading some of the information about the composition, do you think that the composer has succeeded in giving us a musical picture of the idea which is mentioned in the title?

3. While we are talking about this composition it is interesting to know that because of his services as head of the Union of Soviet Composers, a group of men who desired to keep together as much of the Russian music as possible, Ippolitov-Ivanov was awarded the Order of the Red Banner in 1934.

COMPARISON

1. How would you describe the differences between the two pieces of music that we have discussed: "Pomp and Circumstance No. 4" and the "Procession of the Sardar"?

2. Are they alike in any way?

3. Which composer uses the stronger rhythms?

4. Which composer has used melodies which are easy to sing?

5. Do the differences between these compositions have anything to do with the differences between the English people and the Russians?

6. Is there any difference in the way these two men have handled the orchestra?

7. Do you think that the difference in the location of the native countries of the composers might have something to do with the way in which they use the instruments?

The term *program music* is given to those compositions which suggest scenes or events. Sometimes the title tells us what the composer had in mind when he wrote the music. At other times there is a subtitle, an explanation, or even a complete story which provides the listener with the necessary idea as to what is taking place in the music. Of course the imagination plays an important part, but usually composers give pretty clear hints as to their ideas and purposes.

1. Can these two marches come under the general heading of *program music*?

2. Does one of these compositions seem to give a clearer description of the scene than the other?

Imagine that you know nothing whatever of the plans of the composers or the titles of these compositions.

Can you suggest scenes, events, and even titles which might be appropriate to the music of each?

2

MUSIC PICTURES OF THREE COUNTRIES

IN READING about people of different countries we may learn a great deal concerning their industries and occupations, their habits and customs. We discover that mountains or plains, fertile valleys or unfruitful, rocky fields, sunshine and warm breezes or cold and severe climate have a positive effect upon the people who live in these different places. For example, in Norway, where life along the fiords[1] (fyôrds) makes everyone familiar with the water, shipbuilding and fishing are common occupations, while in more southerly countries the habits, customs, and occupations of the people are more likely to be influenced by life on plantations and farm lands.

FOLK SONG

All nations and races have songs which belong to them. Among the various kinds are songs of occupations—songs of the sailor, the soldier, the lumberman, or the worker in the field. The lullaby sung by a mother in the Orient or in Europe means the same thing to her as a lullaby does to a mother in our country; and people all over the world have their own songs to express their special joys or sorrows.

1. Do you remember when you first heard the term *folk song*?
2. Can you explain what it means?

Many times the persons who made up the folk tunes are either unknown or forgotten, and the songs are remembered and sung only by those who have heard them. Then, too, some folk tunes are not the work of any one person. Songs of this kind almost always are the natural musical expression of a mass of people and for this reason are called *folk songs*. For folk songs are like Topsy, — they "never was borned," they "just growed." They are not a bit like the songs which someone has written, someone who is a skilled composer and wishes to write a song of unusual beauty. These may be called *art songs*. It sometimes happens, however, that composers write songs which are so simple and have such a direct appeal that they become very popular and often people think of them as folk songs. "Old Folks at Home" and "My Old Kentucky Home," by Stephen Foster, belong in this group.

Not all folk melodies have words; sometimes they are folk-dance tunes. Many of these dance tunes or melodies have special features that closely

[1] A narrow inlet of the sea with high, rocky shores on either side is called a fiord.

connect them with some particular race or country, and anyone who has learned to notice some of these rhythmic or melodic features may be able to recognize quite easily the nationality from which they come.

Norwegian Dance No. 2 [V. R. G 541 B

EDVARD GRIEG (1843–1907), Norwegian composer. *Living in America at the same time:* WILLIAM H. MCKINLEY.

There is hardly a person who has not heard of the "Land of the Midnight Sun," where from May 13 to July 29 the sun does not set. But things usually even up, and during two of the winter months the days are dark. This is the region of the North Cape and is a part of Norway. Here are deep forests, high mountains, an uneven and rocky coast line, much waste land, and bleak, cold winters.

The Norwegians are a happy people, however, and their poems and ballads (poems which tell a story and can be used for singing) tell of the bravery and daring of these hardy men of the north, who long ago were called Norsemen. Some of the tales are based on fact and some are merely fables. The Norwegians have a large number of these stories, which have been handed down through the years, and the people still love to hear them.

What are some of the things you might expect to find in music which comes from such a country as this?

THE COMPOSER

Norway has reason to be proud of the names of many of her citizens who have really given a great deal to literature and music. Right at the top among these names is that of Edvard Grieg (grēg). Troldhaugen (trôld′ hou-gĕn), which means "hill-sprite" (*sprite* is another name for an elf), was the name of his house, which was located on the beautiful Hardanger (här′däng-ẽr) fiord.

The composer worked in a tiny cabin perched like a bird's nest in the rocks. His study was just big enough to hold a piano and a fireplace. From his window he looked out on one of those gorgeous Norwegian scenes: the fiord, the slopes covered with pines, or maybe a dashing waterfall, and beyond a snowcapped mountain peak.

Alone in his pinewood cabin, he entertained elves, witches, and other funny little creatures. In the wind he heard the voices of the old Norse[1] gods, and in the mists he saw the shapes of ancient heroes. The whole

[1] Norse means "belonging to ancient Scandinavia" (skăn′dĭ-nā′vĭ-ȧ), the land of the Northman.

countryside was filled with folk tales and also with folk music. There were songs of plows and reapers, and there was music of country dances and wedding ceremonies.

Because of all this, Grieg came to know and love the music of his own people, the Norwegian folk song, with its simple style and unaffected sincerity, and he used it in his compositions. Everything he wrote was colored with this clear and fresh Norwegian feeling. He was very successful in writing short instrumental pieces and songs, and in all of them it is easy to discover the national quality of Norwegian folk music.

THE MUSIC

One of the greatest charms of a beautiful melody is simplicity. In order to be simple there must not be too much rhythmic action, for that may prove overexciting. If there are too long intervals* or too many ornamental and unusual designs in the movement of the tones as they follow each other we may become restless. Too many changes in the harmony,* always trying for new and perhaps strange effects, may puzzle us and mix us all up.

Possibly one reason why so many composers use folk tunes in their compositions, while others have molded their original melodies in the naïve (meaning frank or simple), direct style of folk music is because they realize that music is just like any other language. If people know what it is all about and understand it, they will enjoy it. But if the musical ideas are hazy and the expression is not clear, people are not interested in listening to such music.

In the "Norwegian Dance No. 2" the first melody is unusually noticeable, for it is heard six times in all.

FIRST MELODY

The opening section of this composition is marked *allegretto tranquillo e grazioso*.*

1. After hearing the music, is the meaning of this term of expression clear to you?

2. Do you think that the players follow the directions as given in the term of expression?

3. Do the three little grace notes* add to the music?

The entire melody, as well as the piano accompaniment,* is given on page 117 of *Adventure* of THE WORLD OF MUSIC. If you have a chance to look at this, you will not only notice the regular order of the rhythmic pattern in the accompaniment, but you will also be able to follow the progress of the tune as it moves on to the end.

The middle section of this "Norwegian Dance" is in the minor mode,* and the tempo,* or rate of speed, is more rapid.

It contains a melody which seems to have two phrases.

SECOND MELODY (FIRST PHRASE)

SECOND MELODY (SECOND PHRASE)

This is marked *allegro*.

Can you explain what *allegro* means?

Although only a part of each melody is given here, in their complete form these melodies express two distinct ideas. The entire melody may be compared to a sentence, and all the "tone sentences" which have something to do with the first idea are grouped together in one section which may be called A. Those tone sentences which belong to the second idea are grouped in another section which may be called B. The first, or A section, is then repeated, but this time the first or principal melody occurs only twice. If we use letters to describe the form of "Norwegian Dance No. 2," the result will be A B A. This arrangement is called three-part song form.*

Though the two principal melodies of this composition are repeated many times, the music has a good deal of variety. For just as we try to keep from using the same words over and over in our written compositions, so the composer may seek to avoid repeating his music exactly by changing the tempo, the volume (or quantity) of tone, the pitch, and the instrumental tone color.*

1. Which of these features has Grieg changed in the repetitions of this dance tune?
2. Which of them remain the same?

DISCUSSION

This composition is very easy to understand. The songlike melody is repeated so many times that after hearing the selection once it is possible to sing or whistle the tune.

Aside from occupational songs and dances, which suggest various kinds of things to do, Norwegian folk music includes also the processionals, or marches, which are unusually numerous in that country; so numerous, in fact, that nearly every province has its own wedding march.

The composer called the music we have heard a "Norwegian Dance."

1. Why is this a suitable title?
2. Could this music be used for marching?
3. If used for dancing, what kind of dance does the rhythm suggest?
4. What makes the first melody more singable than the second?
5. Do you think the difference in the music of the second section makes the composition more enjoyable?
6. Is there anything in the music that seems especially Norwegian, or could it suggest some other country?
7. Is it what you expected a Norwegian folk dance would be?

FROM NORTH TO SOUTH

In Spain it is hard to separate the song from the dance, for almost all Spanish folk songs are based on dance rhythms.

1. Can you suggest some ways in which Spanish folk music might differ from that of Norway?
2. What could be some reasons for these differences?

GYPSIES

It is natural to think of gypsies when we think of Spain, and Spanish music often follows the rhythm of the music of the gypsies. Russia and Hungary, too, have many songs and dances in which some of the qualities of the gypsy can be noticed.

Because gypsies themselves are free, wandering from place to place and making their homes in forest, by the river, or on the hillside, they find pleasure in simple things, and music to them is as natural as the air they breathe. In Spain the guitar* is one of their favorite instruments and is always a part of their performance. In all gypsy music there are sudden changes of mood from low spirits and even sadness to joy and merriment; from slow movement to rapid, vigorous action; from gentleness to wild delight.

Amelia Josephine Burr, an American writer who lives in New Jersey, has given us a very clear word picture of these care-free, happy-go-lucky people in the following poem:

Romany Gold

There's a cradle of brown on the leaf's crisp edge
And the goldenrod blooms have begun to feather,
We're two jolly vagabonds under a hedge
By the dusty road together.

Could an emperor boast such a house as ours,
The sky for a roof and for a couch the clover?
Does he sleep as well under silken flowers
As we, when the day is over?

He sits at ease at his table fine
With the richest of meat and drink before him,
I eat my crust with your hand in mine,
And your eyes are cups of a stronger wine
Than any his steward can pour him.

What if the autumn days grow cold?
Under one cloak we can brave the weather.
A comrade's troth is the Romany gold
And we're taking the road together.

For many of us there seems to be something very attractive in the free life of the gypsy, whether we see it pictured on the screen or on the stage, or hear it described in a song.

Can you name the titles of any songs about gypsies?

Probably no other people express their character so clearly in their manner of living as do the gypsies.

1. Have you read any stories about them?
2. Can you tell any interesting things about them as a race, their habits, customs, or even their personal traits?

Many composers have found the gypsy tunes very attractive and have used them in their compositions. One of these was a French composer named Chabrier (shä'bryā'). When he was traveling through Spain, he found the music of that country so interesting and colorful that he wrote down many of the Spanish melodies and later used some of them in his compositions.

España[1]

[V. R. 4375 A, B

ALEXIS EMMANUEL CHABRIER (1841–1894), French composer. *Living in America at the same time:* JOHN GREENLEAF WHITTIER.

THE DANCE RHYTHMS

There are two dance rhythms which are especially noticeable in this piece of music. One is full of energy and rapid, the other moves more smoothly and slowly. The quieter one is named "Jota" (hō′tä); it came from the Moors. In this Spanish dance the dancers almost always sing the tune and accompany themselves with guitars and castanets, playing as they dance.

The name of the other dance is "Malagueña" (mä-lä-gān′yä), and it takes its name from the Spanish city of Málaga (mä′lä-gä) on the Mediterranean. This city was dominated by the Moors for a great many years. The dance has few or none of the characteristics of gypsy dances, but is usually danced with mantilla (a kind of veil worn by Spanish women) and fan, and is a good deal like the fandango.* Both the "Jota" and "Malagueña" are in triple measure, each measure having three beats. The slight rhythmic difference between the two dances is easily recognized.

THE ARRANGEMENT OF THE MELODIES

España (ĕs-pä′nyä) follows no fixed form. It is simply a series of dance tunes which the composer has arranged in an artistic and skillful way.

The introduction,* or group of opening measures, gives a clear idea of the rhythm and sets the tempo for the first melody.

FIRST MELODY (MALAGUEÑA)

This melody is repeated three times, and then the second and more lyric melody is heard.

SECOND MELODY (JOTA)

[1] On the Victor record for this selection the title appears as *España Rapsodie.*

THIRD MELODY

FOURTH MELODY

These four melodies follow each other quickly, one after the other, and then after a short period the trombones play a theme which is said to be the only one in this composition which was actually invented by the composer.

FIFTH MELODY

In repeating these melodies the composer changes the effects by using different instruments in the accompaniment, as well as in the melody. Near the close of the composition the first melody is heard again and answered by the trombone theme. As the "Rapsodie" (răp-sō-dē′) ends we hear once more the rhythmic pattern which was heard in the introduction.

THE COMPOSER

Chabrier was one of the most amazing and lovable of composers. He was small, very fat, and had a keen sense of humor. Everything about him attracted attention: his coats, queer hats, strange-colored vests (they were called waistcoats in his time), manner of talking, and elaborate motions of his hands. Everywhere he went he was surrounded by happiness. He had wonderful skill on the piano, and the things he could do with his left hand were amazing. It is no wonder that his compositions are very brilliant and that the harmonies and rhythms seem actually to sparkle.

Chabrier has used the orchestral instruments in such a way as to suggest shining color effects. Strings, bassoons, oboes, French horns, and trombones play the melodies for the most part, while pizzicato* strings and castanets in the accompaniment give a real Spanish feeling. The changes in the instrumental tone color in which the different melodies are played add to our enjoyment of the gaiety and life of this Spanish music written by a French composer.

DISCUSSION

The title of this composition gives an idea as to the kind of music it is. *España* immediately suggests Spain, while the subtitle *Rapsodie* suggests the freedom of an instrumental fantasia,* a type of composition which often uses national melodies in its themes.

1. After hearing the music, can you mention some of the features which suggest the country from which it comes?
2. Can any of these dance tunes be sung?
3. If people dance to this music will they dance with energy? with grace? with rapid or slow movements?
4. How does the first melody differ from the others?
5. Name some of the things in this music which appeal to you more than others.

In *España* some of the melodies are repeated several times.

1. Do these repeated melodies seem more or less interesting than those of the "Norwegian Dance No. 2"?
2. Why?
3. Why do you think composers repeat melodies?

FROM SPAIN TO THE NEAR EAST

When we were reading about the "Procession of the Sardar" on page 8, we found some information about the mountainous country between the Black Sea and the Caspian Sea. In order to understand this next music picture it will be helpful to review this information.

In the Village [V. R. 11883 B

MICHAEL IPPOLITOV-IVANOV (1859–1935), Russian composer. *Living in America at the same time:* CHARLES EVANS HUGHES.

"In the Village" is one of the four short compositions known as *Caucasian Sketches*. The title of this sketch suggests a scene in one of the small towns in the province of Georgia, in the Caucasus (page 8). It was to this province that the composer Ippolitov-Ivanov went, at the time of the World War, to become director of the music school and conductor of the symphony orchestra* in the city of Tiflis (tyē-flyēs′). He found Tiflis a delightful city set high up in the hills on the banks of the Kura (kōō′rȧ) River. In the native district were markets and shops, where Georgian workmen carried on their trades and the air was filled with cries of Persian merchants. This gave the city a colorful blending of the Orient and the hardy Russia of the Czars. "Czar" (zär) was the title of the former rulers of Russia.

For ten years Ippolitov-Ivanov explored the mysteries of Georgian folk music (page 8); he became a famous authority on it. As a result of his search and study of the native music he composed the set of pieces known as *Caucasian Sketches.* Through this work he drew the attention of the entire music world to the attractive rhythms and melodies of these regions so far away.

THE MUSIC

The introduction, which is different from those to which we are accustomed, immediately makes us think of an Oriental scene where people are moving about in strange costumes. These opening measures are similar to a recitative, which in music means a recitation or speech, whether it is uttered by voices or suggested by instruments. Indeed, it sounds as though the instruments were talking with each other.

This is followed by a graceful dance in which the rhythmic figure:

is repeated over and over again. The constant beat of the Oriental drum is heard along with it.

The dance ends, and once more we hear the music of the measures of the introduction, followed by some very soft chords which bring this Oriental sketch to a close.

THE MELODIES

In this music the composer weaves his melodies and rhythms so finely into the general pattern of the whole that they seem to lose their own special character and simply add to the general effect. It is interesting, however, to see how these melodies look and perhaps to play or sing them.

FIRST SECTION (FIRST MELODY)

English horn answered by the muted viola

FIRST SECTION (SECOND MELODY)

English horn accompanied first by viola, then by cello and bass

In the opening melody of the first section it is interesting to notice how the English horn seems to merge into the viola before we are aware of the fact that the melodic phrase is being played by a different instrument. This is all the more unusual because the English horn belongs to the woodwind choir,* while the viola is a member of the string group.

DANCE SECTION (FIRST MELODY)

Oboe accompanied by plucked strings, Oriental drums, and triangle.

DANCE SECTION (SECOND MELODY)

Perhaps you have already noticed that the second melody is only a very little different from the first one. Numbers have been placed under the measures in order to show in what places the second melody is similar to the first one. By comparing measures having the same numbers it is easy to see which ones are repeated.

On the score* the word over the first measure is *Cadenza.* This word is used to describe an ornamental passage for one instrument, usually played without any accompaniment. After the first melody of this cadenza section has been repeated, we hear a more songlike but rather sad melody, the second in the cadenza section. After a time it moves into the first melody again.

Now the measure changes from duple,* in which a strong accent is followed by one weak accent, to triple* measure, in which a strong accent is followed by two weak ones. This is the dance section.

The rhythm of the first few notes of the cadenza section seems to keep right on going, even in the accompaniment for the melodies in the dance section. The first and second melodies of the dance follow each other about, and the way they seem to answer each other makes the music more interesting.

At the end of the dance section the first melody, the recitative,* is heard again. So there is an effect of form, although this is a musical picture. For music, like pictures, must have some plan or form, and "In the Village" seems to be in three-part song form (page 16), even though some melodies, such as the second in the cadenza section, may not be repeated.

A SUMMARY

These *Caucasian Sketches* (we have heard two of them) are like chapters in a story, or short stories, which we read. Each one may be complete in itself, even though the scenes and characters may be the same for all of them. After hearing and talking about the "Procession of the Sardar" there will be no difficulty in finding similar things in this second number of the suite.

But when we compare the music of "In the Village" with that of "Norwegian Dance No. 2" and *España*, probably we shall see many things which are different. The influence of the location of the different countries, as well as that of the habits and manners of the people, will stand out more clearly.

1. How do these three compositions differ in rhythm?
2. Do these rhythms suggest any differences between the countries from which they come?
3. Do the rhythms of each piece seem to belong to one special country?
4. What are the orchestral instruments which seem to be the most used in each of the selections?
5. Would it be possible for you to tell from what country each of these selections has come merely by hearing the music, and without knowing the titles or having any information about it?
6. Which do you notice more in the music of "In the Village," the melody or the rhythm?
7. Does each of these three selections have some special quality that is outstanding?
8. If so, can you find one word to describe it?

3

STORIES IN MUSIC AND DANCE OR MUSIC OF THE BALLET

DANCING is one of the favorite kinds of amusement of people young and old all over the world. Not only do people enjoy ordinary dancing, but folk dancing also is popular. Every year programs of folk music (these are called festivals) are held in many places, and songs and dances of different nations are presented with native costumes and suitable scenery. This makes the performances very effective, and both the dancers and the audience have a great deal of pleasure.

Not only do we enjoy dancing ourselves, but sometimes we like to watch other people dance. Many become expert in the art of dancing and travel about giving special programs, or dance recitals. Often these skillful performers organize into groups and present their dances together. This is known as a *ballet* (băl′ā). Because such a large number of people enjoy ballet dancing it has become one of the most popular forms of entertainment.

Can you give the name of one important ballet company that has presented programs in the United States?

There is nothing new about dancing, although there are always new kinds of dances; for the art of dancing is as old as the world, and our enjoyment of it does not differ from that of people who lived centuries ago.

In very early times, however, much of the dancing was more serious than most of it is now. In those days people used the dance to express their religious feeling as well as their joy in home celebrations. Frequently the dance was included in tragic plays and serious drama as well as in comedies.

Suppose you were going to make up a dance to express sorrow or something quite tragic and then were to make up a dance showing great joy.

1. What difference would you make in the speed of these two dances?
2. How would you change your postures and physical motions to suggest these two different moods?

Since the dancing in the early plays needed music which was suitable to both the dance and the play, a combination of the music and the story slowly developed through a long period of years, centuries in fact, until some plays were set entirely to music. These are known today as operas,* and *opera* is just another name for *music drama.*

Many of these operas have a ballet, that is, special dancing features, and these usually are performed by groups of specially trained ballet dancers. Naturally these operas include the kind of dancing which was popular at the time the operas were written.

What is one of the most graceful dances a present-day composer might put into an opera?

It is important to remember that people enjoy seeing performances given by either one dancer alone or a large group, just as they enjoy hearing concerts given by instrumental or vocal performers, whether soloists or large groups.

When a large group of dancers performs together, the organization is known as a *corps de ballet* (kôr dê băl′ā), or simply as a *ballet*. When a large group of instrumental players performs together, the organization is known as an orchestra. An orchestra usually accompanies the ballet dancers, and in many cases the music is so pleasing that it often is played as a separate concert piece.

Ballet dances may be founded upon a story. Sometimes, however, the dancers merely group themselves into a set of graceful moving patterns which it is enjoyable to see.

Have you ever watched the band of a school or college march on a football field? This may be compared to the second kind of ballet, for sometimes the band merely forms some pattern, such as a cartwheel or a star or perhaps a diamond. These formations tell no story, but just the same they are interesting; and, of course, part of the excitement is in the rhythmic motions which are used.

But when the formation of the band spells the letter of its school or the opponent's school, that means something definite, just as the ballet does when it pictures a story through its dancing. The letter says many things to you which are not actually written on the football field, just as the dancing may suggest many ideas that are not really acted on the stage.

Often the ballet goes further than this, and resembles a kind of speechless acting in which the motions of the actors have been transformed into the graceful and rhythmic movements of the dance.

It is not necessary for a ballet to be a part of an opera in order to tell a story, for composers often have planned ballets which (with or without a story) are complete in themselves. Many writers of music have found suggestions for their compositions in legends and fairy tales for any ideas which quicken the imagination or appeal to the fancy seem to be especially appropriate to ballet music. One of the most popular of these ballets is *Coppélia* (kô-pā′lyȧ).

Photo by Leo S. Pavelle

Graceful Motion and Dainty Costumes Are Important Features in Ballet Dancing

Luis Marquez

It Is No Wonder that Chabrier and Other Composers Found Spanish Customs and Rhythms So Fascinating and Full of Color that They Included Some of Them in Their Original Compositions

Entr'acte and Valse from the Ballet *Coppélia* [V. R. G 511 A

CLÉMENT LÉO DELIBES (1836–1891), French composer. *Living in America at the same time:* JAMES A. GARFIELD.

There are things in the title of this composition which seem to need explanation. *Entr'acte** (äɴ-trăkt'), *valse** (vȧls), and *ballet** can be used with other pieces of music. But *Coppélia* belongs to this music alone, and it means "The Girl with the Enameled Eyes."

Many years ago, so the story goes, in a little Austrian village there lived a maker of toys, Coppelius by name. He liked better than everything else to make dolls, and one day he decided to play a joke on his neighbors. After completing his work on one of the dolls, he dressed it carefully and put it in the window.

Many of the villagers, passing by, wondered who the lovely girl might be. By and by a young fellow, Franz (frȧnts) by name, came along. Seeing the pretty stranger he stopped, smiled, and bowed to her. But she paid no attention to him. Swanhilda (sfän-hĭl'dȧ), a young girl who was very fond of Franz, saw his efforts to get the attention of the girl in the window and was very angry. She made up her mind to find out who this charming creature might be.

Entering the house secretly, she discovered that Coppélia was only a mechanical doll. Quickly changing into Coppélia's clothes, the village maiden began to dance. First she danced a waltz, the music we are going to hear, then two or three other dances. Before long the people, and Franz was among them, discovered that a joke had been played on them and that Coppélia was nothing more than a doll. Franz and Swanhilda made up their quarrel and the day ended happily for everybody.

THE MUSIC

The waltz to which Swanhilda dances opens with an introduction.* Although it is quite short it deserves some attention, for it is in duple rhythm, which is a bit different from the triple rhythm of the waltz. As the introduction comes to a close, the music shifts to waltz rhythm and the first melody is heard.

Violins] FIRST MELODY

The second melody is in a different key.

SECOND MELODY

Wood winds and strings]

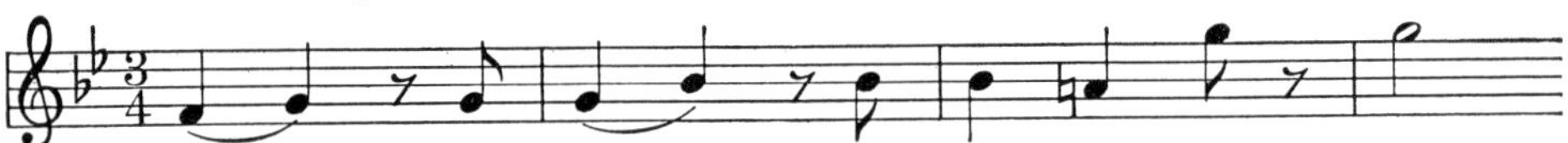

A short interlude* follows, and leads directly into a repetition of the first melody. It seems as though the composer considered this melody more important than the second, for it is heard five times, while the second melody is heard only twice.

As though he wished to put something at the end to balance the introduction at the beginning, Delibes (dê-lēb′) has added some measures in which there is a new melody that is quite different from the two principal melodies. This passage has the effect of a coda, and it brings the "Entr'acte and Valse" to a close with no slowing up of the tempo or lessening of the strength of tone.

If we call the first melody A and the second melody B, can you arrange the letters one after the other as the melodies are heard?

INSTRUMENTS

With the exception of a few measures in the introduction, where the trumpet plays smooth, continuous tones, the string and woodwind choirs* are used almost entirely. This use of delicate instruments seems most fitting in picturing the events which Delibes has chosen to paint in this ballet music.

THE COMPOSER

One of the first landmarks by which the visitor to Paris locates himself is the church of the Madeleine. As a boy Delibes sang in the choir of this famous church. Later he played the organ in several of the other big churches in the French capital, but his real interest was in the theater.

He had a position as accompanist to the *Opéra* (ô-pā-rä′) (the famous opera house in Paris), which meant that he played for the different rehearsals; so he had a wonderful opportunity to study the music of the stage and ballets. When some music for a new ballet was needed he was asked to write it, and his gay rhythmic melodies instantly "caught on."

In 1870, just at the beginning of the Franco-Prussian war, Delibes was asked to write music for an entire ballet. "The Sandman," a story by E. T. A. Hoffmann (perhaps some day you will hear the music of *The Tales of Hoffmann,* by Offenbach (ôf′ĕn-bäk)), appealed to him, for it was a clever little story, with opportunity for many charming dances. *Coppélia* is based on this story, and the "Valse" is one of the most popular waltz melodies in the world. Delibes wrote this ballet music to be danced by trained performers to please an audience, and it has all the grace and charm that awaken the desire to dance. After hearing it you do not wonder that his music delighted French audiences and still remains popular.

SOME THINGS TO THINK ABOUT

Although this piece of music is one of a group of three compositions we are considering together, you may wish to think about this ballet waltz as a separate musical selection.

1. If you should hear this music without knowing the title, would you connect it with dancing?
2. Is the melody easy to sing?
3. Suggest some ways in which dancers might express the mood of the music.

Ballet Music from *Faust* [V.R. G 540 B

CHARLES FRANÇOIS GOUNOD (1818–1893), French composer. *Living in America at the same time:* JAMES RUSSELL LOWELL.

Not only have the French people produced very charming ballets, such as *Coppélia*, but the ballet is a most important part of the opera in France.

The ballet came into France from Italy about the middle of the sixteenth century, more than fifty years before the first English colony was settled on the American continent. The ballet seems to belong especially to the French, although it has an important place in other countries. Kings like Louis XIV made it an important feature in the life at the court. Later, great composers such as Lully (lü-lĭ′) and Rameau (rȧ-mō′) introduced it into the theater, and a great deal of beautiful music has been written for it.

At first the ballet was danced solely by men; later, women were allowed to take part. This kind of dancing became very popular, and today many people in France consider the ballet so necessary in an opera that they will not attend an operatic performance unless it has a ballet. All French opera houses have their *corps de ballet.*

When Gounod (gōō′nō′) was writing his music, although the French had lost a good deal of their enthusiasm for ballet, audiences still liked to see dancing between the acts of the operas. So in the opera *Faust* (foust) Gounod placed a ballet between the fourth and fifth acts.

STORY OF GOUNOD'S BALLET

As this ballet has nothing to do with characters or scenes in the opera itself, it is not necessary to review the story of the dramatic poem by the famous German poet Goethe (gû'tĕ), upon which the opera is based. The ballet, however, has a title of its own. It is called *Walpurgis* (väl-pŏŏr'gĭs) *Night.*

Walpurgis was a saint of the eighth century. Her festival was on the eve of May Day. According to a strange belief of the Germans, this was the occasion for a witches' celebration on the Brocken (brŏk'ĕn), a peak in the Harz (härts) Mountains; and the entire ballet pictures the wild and merry actions of these witches, African slaves, and many weird creatures. There are seven different dances in the ballet. Gounod took some of the melodies from the opera and changed them to make the ballet a clearer picture of the witches and the things they do. We are going to hear only two dances from the ballet at this time.

DANCE OF THE NUBIANS

The first dance, in waltz rhythm, is called "Dance of the Nubians" (or African slaves). Following an introduction, which opens *fortissimo,** a graceful and songlike melody, the first one, is heard.

The next section, in which the second melody is heard, has more variety, for the melody begins in soprano instruments and is answered by lower instruments. Even the accompaniment has a little tune of its own, called a countermelody.*

A FEW DETAILS

The introduction is really a fanfare* of brass and percussion* instruments. The principal melody, played by strings, is repeated and is followed by the second melody. The first melody returns in a different key from that in which we heard it at the beginning. Also there are some slight changes in the instruments which bring a pleasing sense of variety. Then the first melody makes its way, or modulates,* back to the original key. A coda, in which there is no outstanding melody, brings the dance to a close.

MUSIC OF THE SECOND DANCE

The second dance has the title "Cleopatra (klē'ō-pā'trȧ) and the Golden Cup." The expression mark for the first dance was *allegretto tempo di valse,* but this one is marked *adagio* and it makes a pleasing contrast.

As you listen to the music, can you suggest some idea as to the meaning of these terms of expression?

An introduction opens this dance, and then a songlike melody in 4/4, or "common," time is heard.

FIRST MELODY

The second melody is lighter and is played somewhat *staccato.**

SECOND MELODY

Following this melody the smooth, singable tune of the first melody is repeated. The short section which closes this dance has some bits of tune which remind us of the first melody. The strings are more in evidence than any other choir, although brass instruments are important in the introduction, and the lighter percussion instruments, such as the triangle, add to the effect.

UNITY AND VARIETY

Two things in the design of a composition are necessary if the form is to be satisfactory. These are *unity* and *variety*. Gounod has given unity to each of these dances by repeating the first section before bringing the composition to a close. He has provided variety in the new material in the second section of each dance. We have already learned that short compositions following this design are said to be in three-part song form.* It is easy to see, therefore, that the form of "Cleopatra and the Golden Cup" is similar to the form of the "Dance of the Nubians," and that both have an introduction and also a coda.

DISCUSSION

When we have an idea to express we use words or draw pictures or even act things out. Musical ideas are expressed through tones, while the ballet expresses its ideas through motions of the body. When music is written for the ballet it is likely that the rhythm will be its most important quality. Since dancing is rhythmic motion, the rhythmic accents should be easy to catch. This is especially true of some very recent ballets, which are accompanied rhythmically by percussion instruments alone or in which the orchestra at times produces sounds which are merely rhythmic, without melody. Many ballets, and this one from *Faust* is one of them, also have tuneful melodies that are pleasing and graceful.

These two dances are not similar in all respects.

Of these two dances of the *Faust* ballet, which suggests some special manner of dancing through its rhythm?

We have already learned that a ballet may tell a story by dancing and acting rather than by speaking or singing.

1. With your slight knowledge of the story behind this ballet, do you believe that the music offers plenty of opportunity for the dancers to interpret the story?

2. Of these two dances, which has the more interesting melody?

3. Does Gounod provide interest and variety in rhythm, in melody, and in his use of instruments?

GOUNOD HIMSELF

While studying in Italy, Gounod became seriously interested in much of the religious music of the old composers; and for a time he thought of becoming a priest. When, therefore, he returned to France he kept on studying with that end in mind. Although he never did become a priest, the refinement and knowledge he gained in his years of study were of great value to him later in his chosen line of work.

His music is very melodic. Most people know some of the tunes from his opera *Faust*, or "Lovely Appear" from his oratorio* *The Redemption*, even though they may never have heard a performance of either of these works.

THE PRIX DE ROME

Gounod was one of those talented young Frenchmen who won the Prix de Rome (prē′ dĕ rôm′) at the Paris Conservatory. This prize was first offered by Louis XIV; it meant that the winner was given four years of study at the French Academy of Fine Arts in Rome, with a certain amount of money for each year, and also excused from military service. Edward MacDowell, the great American composer, later organized an American Academy in Rome, which provides the same opportunities for American students.

SOME COMPARISONS

In comparing the three compositions,—the "Entr'acte and Valse" from *Coppélia*, by Delibes, and the two selections from the ballet music from *Faust*, by Gounod,—it may be interesting to note

1. The differences in the rhythm.
2. The compositions which suggest dancing and those which seem more songlike.
3. Whether there are any two compositions so similar that one might be substituted for the other.
4. Whether any of these pieces of music sound as though they came from some particular part of the world.
5. In what ways the music for these dances differs from that which we are accustomed to hear today.
6. Whether you like one selection better than the others, and why.

In considering these compositions you have learned a good many new words. If you make a list of them and opposite each give some idea of the meaning, you will find it very helpful when you listen to other musical compositions.

4

DANCES NEW AND OLD

DANCE music has been written by almost every important composer. George Gershwin, the modern American, and Johann Strauss (yō'hăn shtrous'), the "Waltz King," wrote no more dance music than did Bach (bäk) and Mozart (mō'tsärt), who lived in the eighteenth century.

In fact, these older composers wrote such attractive dance music that people still like to hear it, even when there is no chance to dance to it. Just as radio orchestras play concert arrangements* of popular tunes, so some of these composers have taken dance music and fixed or arranged it so that it pleases an audience when played on a concert program. Some writers of music take dance rhythms and use them in their compositions, while still others have used the ballet music from their own or others' operas and made their concert pieces out of that.

Richard Strauss (not a relative of Johann) did this with the waltzes that occur in his opera *Der Rosenkavalier* (dâr rō'zĕn-kä-vä-lēr'). These are so beautiful, and people enjoy them so much when they hear them in the performance of the opera, that the composer has made a concert arrangement of them.

Selected Waltzes from *Der Rosenkavalier* [V. R. G 505 B

RICHARD STRAUSS (1864–), German composer.

Der Rosenkavalier means "The Knight of the Rose" and is the title of a comic opera* in three acts.

The opera takes its name from a custom at the Viennese court of choosing a "Knight of the Rose," who is to serve as a messenger and present a silver rose to a lady in the interest of the noble lover who wishes to marry her. In this opera story a certain baron is in love with the young and beautiful Sophie, daughter of a wealthy but rather ordinary family. The young count, Octavian, is selected to bear the rose, but it is another case of John Alden and Priscilla. Octavian falls in love with the girl, and many funny situations arise.

The dances we are to hear are only a few of those which occur in various places in the opera.

THE COMPOSER

Richard Strauss's favorite composer is Mozart, and in composing *Der Rosenkavalier* Strauss used Mozart's music as his pattern. His success is plain to see, for the graceful, expressive, and singable quality of the music and the liveliness of the story remind us of Mozart's opera *The Marriage of Figaro* (fĭg'ȧ-rō) (page 119).

It is interesting to discover that both Strauss and Mozart wrote most of their music in or near Vienna. Later on we shall be able to compare the music of these two composers. As a matter of fact Vienna was a center of musical interest and activity for a great many years.

People who have written about Richard Strauss describe him as a most easygoing person, enjoying especially his family life in his vacation home in the Bavarian Alps, not far from Munich (mū'nĭk). He is tall and slender and has kindly blue eyes. He is very fond of games, but his taste in all things is simple. It is not easy to understand this, because many people think that his music is difficult and hard to comprehend.

When he is composing he puts down different ideas on loose sheets and places them in a closet, so he tells us, "just as people put their savings in a bank. With the passing of time, the interest or profit accumulates. In the same way time flies, the ideas put down on paper develop within me. One fine day I take all the sheets out of the closet, and an opera grows out of it."

THE MUSIC

The waltzes from *Der Rosenkavalier* are very tuneful; their rhythms are graceful and happy, and the orchestration sparkles. Strange and unusual instrumental effects are often found in the music of Richard Strauss, for not only has he added new instruments to his orchestra but he has developed some new effects with the older ones. He is generally considered as one of the greatest masters of the orchestra because of the way he uses it. It is said that he loves to have "the trombone play like a piccolo," for he has written music that calls for the greatest limits of the pitch range* of many instruments.

In places Strauss has used in his orchestra some sounds that are not truly musical. This is a common habit with writers who have in mind the modern orchestra. In one composition he calls for a wind machine as a part of the orchestra, while in another he uses cowbells as a percussion* instrument. In his opera *Electra* (ē-lĕk'trȧ) he wanted a scream so terrible that no human voice could produce it, so he invented an instrument to make this fearful sound in the orchestra.

These waltzes, however, do not have any such unpleasant effects. In fact they show us how beautifully Strauss can use the instruments of the orchestra when he chooses.

As we listen to the music the following melody is heard immediately:

FIRST MELODY

Because the music moves rapidly and the volume of tone is full we feel at once that the music is happy and full of life. The swaying rhythm of the waltz is recognized at once.

Another melody in the same key provides a happy change, with staccato* effects in the strings.

SECOND MELODY

The key changes as the third section brings in new melodies. Very lively at first, this section moves into a passage of quiet beauty. There is a short interlude in which the following melodic pattern occurs six times.

This melodic pattern, or motive,* is repeated and gives us an idea that the composition is about to end, but the entire orchestra now joins in a tune even more beautiful than the others. Many people consider this the most beautiful of the waltzes of Richard Strauss.

FOURTH MELODY

1. Which of these waltzes seems to be the most spirited?
2. Which is the most graceful?
3. Do you think these waltzes from *Der Rosenkavalier* could be used for dancing at a party?

THE MINUET

While the waltz has long been one of the favorite dances, it has never been more popular than the minuet* was, a century and a half ago. Just as we find that the waltz is a popular dance both in the ballet and out of it, so the minuet was danced both in the early ballet and in the gay social affairs of court life in the eighteenth century.

Today, if we wish music for dancing we only have to turn the dial of our radio and get it. When our country was very young and there were no radios or phonographs, any people who wished to have orchestras to play for the dancing at their parties had to hire them.

In Europe people had not only to hire orchestras but also to engage composers to write their dance music especially for them. In fact, music was ordered for these social affairs in much the same way that refreshments are ordered nowadays. Under these circumstances it is not strange that some of the compositions were much better than others.

One composer who received such orders for music was the famous Mozart (mō'tsärt). That is one reason why we have these "German Dances," which really are minuets.

Four German Dances

[V.R. 1723 A, B

WOLFGANG AMADEUS MOZART (1756–1791), Austrian composer. *Living in America at the same time:* ALEXANDER HAMILTON.

A LITTLE ABOUT THE COMPOSER

Although Mozart was one of the world's greatest composers, who wrote many serious and important works, including symphonies and operas,* he was called upon very often to compose dance music for the special social affairs given by wealthy people in Vienna, where he lived. It came about in this manner:

The court of Austria was located in Vienna, and Emperor Joseph, who ruled the country during Mozart's lifetime, was one of the best customers of this gifted musician. But he was a strange person, this Emperor Joseph, and often went back on his word. At one time he might allow Mozart to live in luxury, while at another the poor composer might not be able to pay his rent. So Mozart made up his mind to try his luck in England and was just about to leave Austria when, in 1787, the Emperor Joseph made him "Dance Composer to the Court" at a salary of about $400 a year — a sum which went much further in those days than it would today.

In his new position Mozart wrote many dances for the court balls. Vienna was famous for these gay occasions, where visiting royal persons were entertained and the ladies of the court wore their latest wigs, ruffles, fans, and buckled slippers.

Among the many sets of dances which Mozart composed at this time are the *Eight German Dances,* of which we are to hear four. They express the happy nature of the composer, while their rhythms are those of the old-fashioned stately dances of the Viennese court of the 1700's.

Although we soon grow tired of much of the dance music which we hear nowadays (some of it lives only a few weeks), this dance music by Mozart still delights those who hear it, even though it is as old as our country, for it was composed in 1790, the year following the inauguration of George Washington as our first President.

Perhaps it is not strange that the compositions of men who lived many years ago continue to be performed and are popular. In many cases, as with the music of Mozart, they express feelings and ideas that are clear, simple, and natural. Everybody likes to hear them.

Some of these master composers began writing when they were quite young. When Mozart was only a little child his father discovered that he had unusual musical talents and so began to train him to play at public concerts. The boy developed unusual skill, and on his concert tours the audiences were astonished because the child composed as well as played much of the music on his program. As time went along he did things that one could hardly expect and became the great musician that such a talented child ought to be. But many times children who can do some things especially well do not amount to much when they grow up. This certainly was not true of Mozart for, although his life was short, he still remains one of the greatest of all composers.

THE MUSIC

Mozart wrote these dances as a group to be played by a small orchestra, so it says on the score.* They are all in 3/4 measure, but although there is no change in the meter,* still there is no lack of interest as one dance follows another.

Most of these dances are divided into three parts, and the design, or pattern, is similar to the three-part song form described on page 16.

Musical designs do not have to follow a fixed rule, however, and great composers such as Mozart do not hesitate to change their musical forms to suit their purposes. As you listen to the music you will notice that Mozart has not used the same form in each dance. That is one reason why these dances are interesting and pleasing to hear.

When Mozart wrote these dances he had some other ideas in mind than simply composing a set of rhythmic pieces. In each number there is a middle section, or *trio section,* as it is called; and to some of these trios he has given titles which suggest his special thought. These are:

In No. 5, "The Canaries"
In No. 6, "The Organ-Grinder"
In No. 8, "The Sleigh Ride"

It will be easier for you to follow the music of these dances as they are played if you can recognize the melodies as they appear and as they are repeated. When you can discover the pattern which is made as these melodies follow one another, you will have discovered the form of this music. Therefore, a few measures of the principal melody (left) and the trio melody (right) of each dance are given here. Sometimes they appear an octave* lower than they actually sound.

In "German Dance" No. 8, Mozart's music calls for real sleigh bells and post horns. The post horn was originally used as a signal for stage-coaches carrying the mail, and is a small brass instrument on which only a few tones can be played.

SOME THINGS TO THINK ABOUT

1. In comparing these four dances what differences do you discover in

   a. tempo? *b.* form? *c.* instruments? *d.* mood?

2. How do these dances differ from those we hear nowadays?
3. Do you prefer any one dance in this group?

4. State your reasons.
5. Can you suggest any kind of school program in which these four dances by Mozart could be used with good effect?
6. How does Mozart's music suggest the meaning of his titles?
7. Do these sections with special titles appeal to you more than those which have none?

A COMPARISON

Many times we find it helpful to compare two pieces of music and our ideas about them. In listening to the four "German Dances" by Mozart we have noticed the differences between them as well as the points in which they are alike.

The waltzes from *Der Rosenkavalier* were written more than one hundred years later than the "German Dances." While today Richard Strauss uses a very large orchestra, sometimes as many as 110 players, the small orchestra of Mozart's day had only violins, violas, cellos, double basses, flutes, oboes, English horn, clarinets, bassoons, horns, trumpets, and tympani.

In addition to the better kind of wind instruments and greater skill in playing, Richard Strauss has had the advantage of new ideas in freedom of form and richness of harmony. In comparing the music by Strauss with the compositions by Mozart it is well to keep these things in mind.

1. Is there any difference between the kinds of dancing suggested by the waltzes from *Der Rosenkavalier* and the four "German Dances"?
2. Do you prefer the orchestra as Mozart used it to that used by Strauss?
3. Would the Strauss orchestra be suited to the Mozart music?
4. Would the Mozart orchestra be suited to the Strauss music?

The answer to this question may show whether Strauss was successful in trying to write music which would be similar in style to Mozart's.

What do you think are the most outstanding differences between these two compositions?

It may be interesting to find more information concerning the changes which have taken place in the progress of music from Mozart's time to that of Richard Strauss, especially in the matter of

a. Orchestras: their size and the variety of instruments.
b. Freedom from following certain set forms.
c. Harmonies which are more interesting because they are unusual.

5

A

MUSIC STORY

IN

EIGHT CHAPTERS

THE experience which you have had in listening to music in which the story is told by dancing and acting has made clear the meaning of the word *ballet.*

You know too that ballet music is often played as a concert number. Here is a set of pieces, called the *Nutcracker Suite,* which is really the music of a ballet. The composer, Tchaikovsky (chī-kŏf'skĭ), has grouped his selections into a suite,* which has such a delightful and natural appeal that you will find it difficult to believe that this music was written to order. Yet such was the case, for in 1891 this popular Russian musician received an invitation to write both an opera and a ballet for performance at the St. Petersburg (now Leningrad) opera house.

He found the story for his ballet in a tale by Hoffmann, the same man who wrote the story for *Coppélia* (page 27).

Nutcracker Suite

[V.R. 8662, 8663, 8664

PETER ILYITCH TCHAIKOVSKY (1840–1893), Russian composer. *Living in America at the same time:* PHILLIPS BROOKS.

THE STORY

Once upon a time there was a little girl who had a wonderful dream on Christmas night in which all of her dolls and toys came to life. The hero of these is her favorite toy, a plain, ordinary nutcracker. Strange things can happen in a fairy tale, and in this one the nutcracker is changed into a handsome prince. He leads the toy soldiers in battle with the Mouse King, who has come with his troops to eat up all the goodies on the Christmas tree.

Prince Nutcracker, victorious, then carries the little girl away to a wonderful spot, Jam Mountain, which is ruled by the Sugar Plum Fairy. By this time our little girl has become a princess, and the Sugar Plum Fairy gives an entertainment for her visitors, in which dances by Chinese, Arabian, and Russian dolls, toy flutes, and the Sugar Plum Fairy take place. At the close all the guests join in a graceful waltz.

RUSSIAN BALLET

The success of this ballet was great, for the music is gay and full of charm. The ballet in Russia was a very popular art. People gave their lives to it, spending long hours in exercises to make them relaxed and grace ful. Little children attended schools of the ballet, in which they learned to make their motions graceful and combine them with artistic costumes and suitable background, or scenery. Much of the music written for the Russian ballet was so lovely that it still lives and is performed as concert music.

MUSIC OF THE SUITE

Eight musical compositions are gathered together in this suite, each separate from the other, yet all held together by the interest of the story. They suggest the scenes and happenings of the tale.

The titles of the different numbers in the suite are:

1. Overture Miniature
2. Marche
3. Dance of the Sugar Plum Fairy
4. Trépak (Russian Dance)
5. Arab Dance
6. Chinese Dance
7. Dance of the Flutes
8. Waltz of the Flowers

The mood of this music is particularly happy. Its melodies, harmonies, and rhythms are charming and varied, and Tchaikovsky has made novel but appropriate use of the different orchestral instruments all the way through. These things add interest to the music, quite apart from its association with the story.

OVERTURE MINIATURE

The word *overture* has two meanings. It may mean a prelude, or introduction to something which follows, such as a ballet, an opera, or a suite, or it may be used as a name for a separate form used by composers, in which there are two themes, which are treated or developed according to certain rules. This overture not only serves as an introduction to the other numbers of the suite but also follows the plan of the classic overture.*

This is just such an overture as one might expect to introduce a musical fairy tale. The music opens with this melody:

FIRST MELODY

This is followed by a passage in which the flute and clarinet seem to be hurrying along on wings. Suddenly a little part of the first melody is heard, after which the violins play a tune marked *dolce cantabile,** which begins like this:

Stokowski and the Philadelphia Symphony Orchestra, Who Play the *Nutcracker Suite*

Listen, Learn, Enjoy—These Pupils Do All Three

SECOND MELODY

All of this is repeated, with wood winds* and strings playing melodies, as well as some rapid scale passages, until pizzicato* chords and a soft tone of the celesta* bring the overture to a close.

MARCHE

Some people have divided this suite into two parts and begin Part II with the "Marche." But in the score, and on the record, the order given here is followed.

The "Marche" opens with a theme, played by the brasses, which seems to strut about as though it were very important.

FIRST MELODY

This melody is heard over and over again, but the repetitions are separated by different themes, or interludes,* in which the music moves back and forth among the different choirs: strings, wood winds, and then brass, adding more and more force and life till the first section of this movement ends.

Some bright running passages for flutes, answered by strings, make up the middle (or second) section, which is much lighter than the first and provides a pleasing contrast.

There is an immediate return to the first melody of the "Marche," and the repetition of the first section is decorated with bright scale passages which seem to dart across the principal melody as the composition closes in a gay and lively manner.

DANCE OF THE SUGAR PLUM FAIRY

It is easy to imagine that music with such a title would be dainty and delicate. It is in this number that Tchaikovsky uses the celesta with best effect. The difference between its light, clear tone and the reedy sound of the bass clarinet, and the suggestion of liveliness in the plucked, or *pizzicato,** strings, illustrate Tchaikovsky's ability in using the orchestral instruments to carry out his ideas.

The "Dance of the Sugar Plum Fairy" has one melody which is heard four times in all and begins as follows:

This dance may not be so lively as some, but it has a beauty all its own.

THE CELESTA

While working on the *Nutcracker Suite* Tchaikovsky left Russia for a tour of Europe and the United States. After appearing in a series of concerts in some American cities, he became homesick for Russia. As he hastened on his way he heard in Paris a new instrument called the *céleste*, or *celesta.* Its tone so delighted him that he ordered one to be sent immediately to his home in Russia. He used this instrument in the *Nutcracker Suite* and it was played for the first time in any orchestra at the *première*, or first performance, of this composition.

The celesta is a small keyboard instrument looking something like a parlor organ. It has a keyboard of five octaves, the notes sounding an octave higher than they are written. The hammers strike steel plates which are placed over wooden boxes which resound, or re-echo, giving the instrument a pure and lovely tone.

TRÉPAK

This is the most Russian music in the suite, since the Trépak was a popular Russian folk dance. Two things which are found in most Russian folk dances* are the accompaniment of hand-clapping and foot-stamping, and a general increase in speed as the dance nears the end.

Opening with a loud chord, the first melody suggests a scene that is gay and full of fun.

FIRST MELODY

This melody occurs four times, with many instruments seeming to compete with each other for first place.

Then a second section follows, in which the rhythmic patterns seem more important than the melodic patterns. The kettledrums and tambourine take turns in beating a rhythm which seems determined to be heard, no matter whether we get tired of it or not.

The first melody returns with renewed force and speed, and the entire orchestra unites in firmly emphasizing the rhythmic pattern.

Only the horns appear to be responsible for expressing a melodic idea. This dance ends in a whirl of excitement.

ARAB DANCE

This piece of music is full of Oriental (page 9) feeling. The mystery and strange attraction of the land of Arabia are suggested in the reedy tone color* of oboes, clarinets, and bassoons, while the uninterrupted droning* in the accompaniment suggests a picture of an Arabian street where shopkeepers with their queer turbans move quietly about as though they were guarding a secret.

Tchaikovsky has used muted* strings and wood winds to paint this musical picture. No brasses are permitted.

There is a short introduction, in which a steady humming in the accompaniment suggests a mood of mystery. There is a weird call from the clarinets, and then the opening melody is heard. There is something dreary and rather mournful about it. The music is marked *molto espressivo.*

FIRST MELODY

The effective use of the tambourine, the wistful appeal of oboe and English horn, the strange shifting from minor to major and back again, which give the music its Oriental feeling, are devices that composers often use when they wish to imitate the music of the East, or to suggest an Eastern scene.

CHINESE DANCE

This dance is only thirty-two measures long, but it is full of imagination and has a certain charm that attracts us. After the rhythm is fixed in a figure that is constantly repeated by the bassoons and double basses (pizzicato), an odd little tune is played by the flutes, and at once there is an impression of a dance that is unusual and rather curious.

The sound of little bells takes turns with a string pizzicato. The low tones of the bassoon and the high tones of the flutes and piccolo suggest the humor of little dancing Chinese dolls. Though it is short, the dance brings the Far East before our imagination; China, with its golden dragons, its high-piled pagodas (Chinese temples), and its queer music. The dance ends suddenly with an abrupt chord.

DANCE OF THE FLUTES

This title is the English for "Danse des Mirlitons" (däns dā mēr'lē-tôn). A *mirliton* is a toy pipe, something like our *kazoo*, and produces a sound much like that made by singing against a comb wrapped in tissue paper. When the ballet was performed originally, mirlitons were used, but flutes take their place in the concert arrangement of the suite. With this title it is to be expected that they are heard more often than any other instruments in this number of the suite.

A brief introduction gives us an idea of the rhythm, and then three flutes play the first melody of this movement.

FIRST MELODY

This melody is repeated after an interlude in which a songlike theme* is played by the English horn. The music is dainty and gay, although once in a while there is a suggestion of dreaminess.

Quite different from this first section, which is full of delicate beauty in rhythm and tone color, is the second section, where the brasses seem to lead the dancers into more lively motion. But the flutes return with the first melody, and this dance ends as happily as it began.

WALTZ OF THE FLOWERS

The introduction to the "Waltz of the Flowers," or "Valse des Fleurs" (våls dā flûr), as it is called in French, is important because of the harp cadenza,* which follows a group of chords that are played by wood winds. Not only is this passage for the harp very bright, but it leads gracefully to the first theme of the waltz, which is played by the horns and is one of Tchaikovsky's loveliest and most famous melodies.

FIRST MELODY

After this melody by the French horns has been repeated, the violins play a new melody:

SECOND MELODY

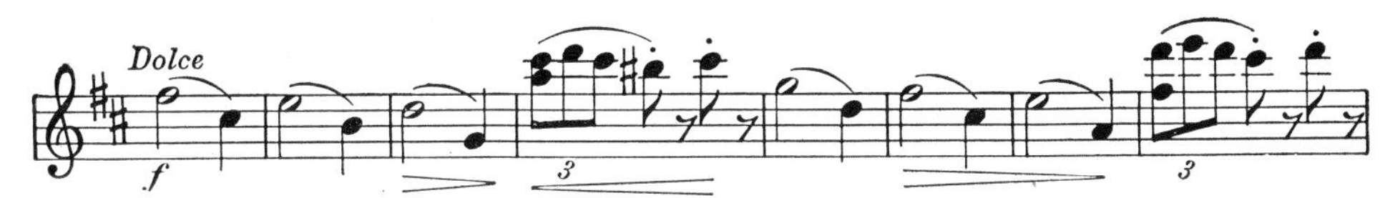

At the end of this section the wood winds introduce another melodic idea:

THIRD MELODY

A melody played by the viola and cello offers a pleasing contrast:

FOURTH MELODY

The design is completed by a return to the third melody, which is played by the strings, and this leads directly into the first and second melodies.

A brilliant coda finishes the final number of the *Nutcracker Suite*. The graceful rhythm, the variety of melody and harmony, and the unusual way in which the instruments are combined in this waltz prove that as a composer of waltzes Tchaikovsky is in the front rank.

WHO WAS TCHAIKOVSKY?

Tchaikovsky's father was a government engineer in charge of a rich mine. His mother was a French woman. They lived in a small and not very attractive town, but the Tchaikovsky home was like a palace, with expensive surroundings and many servants.

Young Peter was taught by a French governess and was very bright. When six years old he could read French and German easily, and at seven was writing verses in French. But he was unusually sensitive. His governess called him a "porcelain" child. It was impossible to scold him, for he became alarmingly upset at the slightest reproof. He carried this sensitive feeling through his whole life, and it caused him a great deal of suffering over small things which ordinary people would never notice.

He began music lessons early, but music had a strange effect upon him, and his family thought it had an unhealthy effect also; and so he was sent to a law school in St. Petersburg. The sole thing for which he was noted at this school was a very poor record in mathematics.

He went to work as a clerk in the Ministry of Justice, one of the government offices, and had an absent-minded habit of tearing off pieces of paper and chewing them. At one time he ate up almost the whole of a very important official paper.

In his spare time Tchaikovsky began to study harmony, and it was not long before he discovered the line of interest for which he was best fitted. Such a sensitive man needed to be alone when he was at work, and he spent long months in the country. He loved Russia with a deep and sincere affection, and put into his music the joys and sorrows, the very spirit of his native people.

CONCLUSIONS

There are different ways to consider this music. You may think of each number as a separate selection, and may form your opinions as to the title and whether it is suitable or not; the melodies and whether they can be sung easily; the variety in the rhythms and harmonies; the tone quality of the instruments, heard alone and with others; and your response to each movement and what it means to you.

Also you may wish to compare the different dances, both for the musical differences and for the things which are common to all of them.

Or you may wish to know about the circumstances which gave to the composer the idea of writing this music, and read the Hoffmann fairy tale. There are many books which tell this story in full.

But in making up your mind and deciding just how you feel about the numbers or dances of this modern suite, you may find some help in considering and answering some of the following questions:

1. Can you form a picture in your mind of the ballet with which this music might be used?

2. How has Tchaikovsky used orchestral instruments to suggest the different nationalities mentioned in the titles?

3. Can you describe any Russian dance?

4. Is the "Trépak" anything like the one you have in mind?

5. Would you call the "Arabian Dance" beautiful music?

6. What appeal does it make to you?

7. Does any number in this suite suggest humor?

8. In what way?

9. Are there any numbers in this suite which do not seem to belong to any special country?

10. How do they differ from the others?

11. Are there any dances which, through their rhythmic patterns, seem to suggest any special steps and motions?

12. Can you disregard the title of this suite,—*Nutcracker*,—and, with the music clearly in mind, plan some kind of performance that will fit the music and yet be up-to-date both in plot and action?

6

SEVENTEENTH-CENTURY MUSIC THAT STILL LIVES

THE word *suite* is not an uncommon one. It can be used in different ways: a suite of rooms; a suite of furniture; or the suite of some important person, meaning his attendants. In each one of these situations the word suggests a group of different things or persons that are connected with or related to each other.

In music the word describes a certain kind of instrumental form. Years ago it meant a set of dances in different rhythms but in the same key* or related keys. The choice and number of dances in a suite depended on the composer's knowledge of the different dances and his artistic judgment. Nowadays we give the word to an instrumental form which is free as to the kind and number of its movements.

What suite do you know, and how are its movements related to each other?

Suite

[V.R. 1664 B

HENRY PURCELL (1658–1695), English composer. *Living in America at the same time:* COTTON MATHER.

THE MUSIC

There are four numbers in this suite, each very short, but each bearing a title.

1. Country Dance
2. Jig
3. Song Tune
4. Canaries

These dances by Purcell (pûr′sĕl) have all the freshness of the English countryside. They are simple and natural, two qualities that are often found in English music.

You will probably enjoy the music much more if you know something about the opening melody of each dance.

1. Country Dance

When you look at these melodies it is easy to see that there are some differences in the time signatures.* The first and third dances are in 3/4, or triple,* measure, and the second and fourth are in 6/8 measure. When you listen to the music you will discover that the second and fourth dances move more rapidly than the others and give the impression of being in duple,* or two-beat, measure.

Another difference which you will notice as you listen to the music is that the first and fourth dances are in the major* mode, while the second and third are minor.*

THE INSTRUMENTS

There were not so many instruments in the orchestra of Purcell's time as there are today, and the names were different. For example, this set of little dances is played by five instruments. This table lists them, with the modern instruments which most nearly resemble the ones used in this suite.

Purcell's Instrumentation	Present-day Instrumentation
Treble viol	Violin
Viola d'amore	Viola
Viola da gamba	Violoncello
Violone	Double bass
Harpsichord	Piano

But even in Purcell's time the older stringed instruments—the *viols**—were slowly giving way to the newer—the *violin* family (violin, viola, cello, and double bass). Purcell himself wrote much for them. King Charles II preferred them, and established a band of twenty-four violins, to which Purcell was official composer. The viols, however, continued to be used by most musicians.

THE PERFORMERS

In this country there is an organization called the "American Society of Ancient Instruments." The purpose of this organization is to perform the music of the seventeenth and eighteenth centuries on the instruments for which it was originally composed. It was founded in 1927 by Ben Stad, and three members of the Stad family play in the group. They not only give programs all over the country, but are also heard over the radio.

Mr. Stad is the director of the group, and this is what he says about his purposes and ideals:

> The famous music of the old masters has always, from my earliest years, been like the whisper of the eternal spirit in my heart. In Rotterdam, the city of my birth, the love of the old music was always with me.
>
> I came to America, and the same beautiful spirit of the ancient harmonies followed me. And here, in this land I can now call mine by adoption, I have tried to give, with the best that is within me, of that voice of music which is the source of whatever we do today that is worth our labor.
>
> Several years ago in Philadelphia we founded the American Society of Ancient Instruments, the first of its kind in America. We revive in our ensemble * the orchestra as it was when the great masters of music Purcell, Bach, Handel, and others wrote their orchestrations.
>
> Always we try to reproduce the old music as it was in its original form and setting. Each year our Society gives a festival, or program, where the performance of the old scores (and sometimes the old dances) crowns our long months of rehearsals, three or four a week through most of the year.
>
> Nothing is built where there are no foundations. The old masters are the deep roots of our art. Unless the roots be well taken care of the branches die and the leaves wither. Our Society is trying to see to the roots so that the growth of today may be to full fruition.

In this record of the suite Ben Stad and his players have used the original orchestral arrangement of the composition.

HENRY PURCELL
AND THE TIMES IN WHICH HE LIVED

Six years before the settlement of New York, Henry Purcell was born in England. Oliver Cromwell died the same year, and Charles II became ruler and king of England. Therefore music again had to depend upon the support of the rich members of royal families.

It was an age when everything was upset both in politics and religion. Migration to the new world, America, was in full swing; and Maryland, Pennsylvania, and the Carolinas were soon to become colonies.

When only six years old, Henry entered the choir of the Royal Chapel, and not only was taught how to sing, but also had lessons on the lute,* viols, and organ.

When he left the choir he went to work for a repairer and tuner of instruments, and in this way he learned the mechanical details of all kinds of wind instruments. Many times he tuned the organ at Westminster Abbey, on which he later was to play and compose. It is not strange, therefore, that Purcell's music has somewhat of a religious feeling.

When he was only eighteen years old, Purcell became composer for the king's violins, the royal band of players, who wore scarlet suits or livery and played at court affairs, as well as for the entertainment of guests at mealtimes.

But when, three years later, he became organist at Westminster Abbey, he was busy from morning till night writing anything that the ceremony of the church needed. He also began to write music for the stage, as well as sonatas* and suites for the strings. During this period he was the bright musical sun in the English sky. At the same time Milton, Dryden, and John Bunyan were making their great contributions in prose and poetry.

COMPARISONS AND DISCUSSION

There are certain things in this music that are similar to music you have already heard. If you recall the "German Dances" by Mozart you may be able to name some ways in which the "Country Dance" of Purcell's suite is like the first of the "German Dances."

It is interesting to note that Mozart called his music a set of dances while Purcell grouped his pieces into a *suite*.

Would it be all right to call the four "German Dances" a suite?

Mozart called the fifth of his dances "Canaries." Purcell gave the same title to the fourth number of his suite.

1. Can you find any places in which these two compositions are alike?
2. To which selection do you think the title is more appropriate?
3. Do any numbers more than others in this suite suggest dancing?
4. Can you describe the kind of dancing which might be used?
5. In what way does the composer carry out the meaning of the title in the third number of this suite?

Although each number of this set of pieces is like a complete paragraph, they are all joined together to form a complete musical chapter.

1. What is your idea about the instrumental effect of this music?
2. Do you think that music like this would sound as well when played by a large modern symphony orchestra as it does when played on five instruments of the seventeenth century?

7

MUSIC AND FAIRY TALES

PROBABLY, at some time or other, everyone has read a fairy story and liked it. Andersen and Grimm are familiar authors of such tales, and we all enjoy roaming about the streets of the "Land of Make-Believe," where strange things may happen, but everything comes out all right in the end.

It is natural, therefore, for composers to read fables and old tales in order to find ideas which they can express effectively in music, for just as composers have used folk dances for designs and folk tunes for themes, so they have used folk tales for ideas. Sometimes their music is accompanied by dancing, and then we have the ballet. The composer may give us a suggestion of what he had in mind when writing the music for a special scene like the "Procession of the Sardar," in which rhythmic patterns and instrumental effects are used to portray the picture. In the ballet or in program music* the listener has to use his imagination to complete the story. At other times composers combine words with music, and an opera results. Without the action and on a far smaller scale it might be an art song.*

If the words are there, as in the opera, then we have no choice but to go along with the composer as he leads us through this scene and that until we come to the end.

Overture to *Hänsel and Gretel* [V. R. 11929 A, B

ENGELBERT HUMPERDINCK (1854–1921), German composer. *Living in America at the same time:* WILLIAM HOWARD TAFT.

The same brothers Grimm who gave us *Snow White and the Seven Dwarfs* also wrote the fairy tale *Hänsel* (hĕn′zĕl) *and Gretel* (grā′tĕl). It was this story which gave to Adelheid (ä′dĕl-hīt), a sister of Humperdinck (ho͝om′-pĕr-dĭngk), the idea of writing a set of little verses for the amusement of her own children. She sent these to her brother and asked him to compose some simple music for them. The verses and music were arranged in the form of a play and on Christmas night were used in an entertainment which Adelheid gave in her home. In the meantime Humperdinck had become so excited over the idea of the play that he persuaded his sister to rearrange it so that it would be suitable for the libretto* of a full-length opera. The opera *Hänsel and Gretel* is the result of the united efforts of Humperdinck and his sister. It has been tremendously popular with old and young alike.

This overture, or prelude, as it is sometimes called, contains many of the delightful melodies used in the opera. Because there is no scenery or action for you to watch as you listen to the music, you will have to imagine a good many things, and the story will help very much. You can picture a broom-maker's cottage, similar to that of the Dwarfs in *Snow White*. In your mind you can see these two children, follow their adventures, and share their experiences.

THE STORY

Once upon a time there was a poor couple — a broom-maker, Peter by name, and his wife, Gertrude. They had two children, a boy named Hänsel and a girl, Gretel.

One day, before Peter and Gertrude went out to sell the brooms they had been making, they gave the children the last bit of bread in the house and told them to work hard cleaning up the rooms and doing various other chores. Hänsel and Gretel did work for a while, but soon they began to get hungry. To keep up their spirits they danced and sang. They were having such a good time! But right in the midst of it all their mother returned, tired and cross, for she had not taken in any money and therefore had brought home nothing to eat.

When she found the children sitting on the floor and making so much noise instead of being at work, she was angry and drove them out into the wood, telling them not to return until they had filled their basket with strawberries. Then she dropped down on a chair and fell asleep from hunger and weariness.

The two children began to pick berries and soon forgot their troubles. But they failed to notice one thing. They were getting deeper and deeper into the wood. Full of fun and mischief they imitated the cuckoo's cry, and because they were hungry they began to eat the strawberries. After a time, to their astonishment, they discovered that the basket was empty.

Meanwhile it had grown very dark, and the children became frightened. They could not find their way out of the wood and wandered helplessly around. The rustling of the trees made them think of ghosts. The birds were still, and only the cuckoo was heard in the far distance.

They settled down under a fir tree to find shelter from the terrors of the night. There the Sandman found them and filled their eyes with sand. But when he had gone away, the children knelt on the soft earth and together recited the prayer their mother had taught them:

Two my head pro-tect-ing, Two my feet di-rect-ing; Two do guard me on the right,

Two up-on my left in sight, Two there are that cov-er, Two a-bove me

hov-er, Two to whom the word is giv'n To guide my steps to heav - en.

Soon they were fast asleep, and the fourteen angels watched over them so that no harm might come to them.

The next morning they were awakened from their dreams by the little Dew Fairy, whose business it is to run over the hills and fields waking up everything that is still slumbering. As he sprinkled the faces of the sleeping children with dew from his bluebell, he sang this song:

I am up with the break of dawn
To greet with joy the golden morn;
I bid the children to arise.
Ding dong! ding dong!
The waking bell is ringing;
The birds begin their singing.
I gather dew from flowers
And scatter this in showers.
Awaken now, the dawn is here;
Be up, enjoy the morning cheer!

The Dew Fairy slipped away before the children could stir. When at last they opened their eyes, what did they see but a little house made of cakes and sugar candy! The smell was so delicious that the hungry children were wild with delight.

They cautiously approached the cottage and, not seeing anybody, broke a piece off the wall. How good it tasted!

Just then a voice in the house called:

Alarmed for a moment, the children soon regained their courage, telling each other that it was

and went on nibbling. But the door of the cottage opened, and an ugly old witch came out. It was she who rode on a broomstick through the air at night; in the daytime she persuaded children to come into her house and then popped them into the oven and made gingerbread of them. Afterward she ate them!

She tried to be friendly with Hänsel and Gretel, but they did not trust her pleasant words and started to run away. Then the witch raised her magic wand, and, swinging it three times to the left and three times to the right, pronounced this spell:

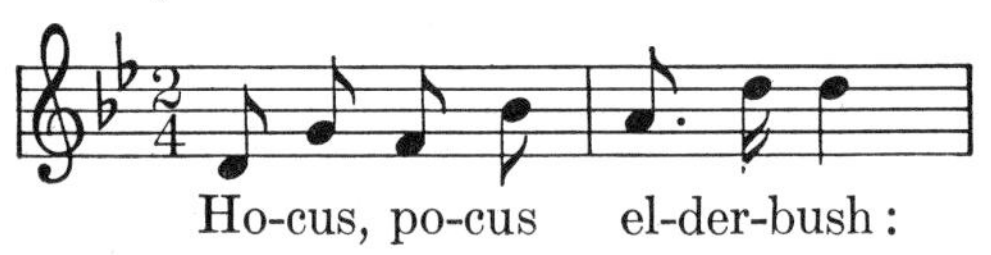

In the overture Humperdinck has turned this tune upside down, like this:

This cast a spell over the children so that they couldn't move. The witch shut Hänsel in the stable and fed him with almonds and raisins to make him fat. When she had done this she was so delighted that she seized a broomstick and rode wildly on it around the room. Then she called Gretel to watch the oven and see when the cakes were done.

But Gretel was smarter than the witch. Pretending to be stupid, she asked the witch to show her how to watch the oven, and the old woman stooped to peep into it. No sooner had she done this than Gretel gave her a push, and in she tumbled. Gretel slammed the door, leaving the witch to bake in her own oven, and after Hänsel was released the children danced around in glee.

American Society of the Ancient Instruments, Who Play the *Suite* by Purcell (Page 50)

Then, with a crash, the magic oven fell to pieces, and lo and behold! all the gingerbread figures which had been standing around were changed into living children. Overjoyed with their liberty, they danced about Hänsel and Gretel, thanking them for having released them from the spell of the old witch. This music is full of their happiness and joy.

Guided by the songs and shouts of the happy gingerbread children, Peter and his wife, who had been searching all night, found Hänsel and Gretel, who rushed into their arms. All sadness and poverty were left behind forever, for in the sugar cottage they found enough to make them rich and happy all the rest of their lives. And so they thanked God, who had taken care of them in their need.

THE MUSIC

In the story of *Hänsel and Gretel* you have found certain melodies as they occur in the opera, and you have been able to connect these melodies with certain events and actions.

The "Overture" contains some of these melodies, and it is interesting to see how Humperdinck has used them. They are heard in this order:

1. The Prayer melody
2. "Hocus Pocus"
3. Song of the Dew Fairy
4. Dance of the Gingerbread Children

Sometimes in the "Overture" these melodies are changed slightly from the way they are sung in the opera. But the likeness is clear enough to permit you to recognize the tunes instantly, especially if you have heard any of them before. The *prayer* melody has been used as the musical signature for a famous radio program broadcast for many years.

A FEW IDEAS ABOUT THE MUSIC

Almost every opera begins with music which is intended to prepare the listener for that which is to follow, or "to set the scene."

1. As long as you are familiar with the story of this opera and have heard the music of the overture, do you think that this music "sets the scene" successfully?

2. If you knew nothing about the story or any of the music of the opera, how would you describe the music of the opening melody of the overture?

3. What are some of the differences in tempo, rhythm, and instruments that you notice when listening to the music?

4. This opera has been very popular. What reasons can you give for this?

SOME MATTERS OF IMPORTANCE

When a musical composition, either long or short, pleases us, and we enjoy listening to it, it is natural that we should be interested in the man who wrote it.

Humperdinck found great delight in the folk songs of his native country, and many of these center about elves and other creatures that exist only in the imagination.

His original melodies are full of the simple charm of folk tales and folk tunes. He selected his subjects with care, and his purpose was to express his own interest and feeling so clearly that others would find his compositions delightful. This may be part of the reason that *Hänsel and Gretel* has been so popular everywhere.

Humperdinck greatly admired Richard Wagner (väg′nẽr), the great German composer of "music dramas*"; and, when a young man, he went to Bayreuth (bī-roit′) to study Wagner's music. Because of this admiration for Wagner and his personal friendship with the composer, Humperdinck has used in his own writing many of Wagner's methods and ideals, and in his *Hänsel and Gretel* there is just as perfect a union of story and music as in any serious music drama. It is a pity that Humperdinck, who had so much talent, did not leave more compositions for our enjoyment.

STORYTELLING

The art of storytelling is as old as the hills, and there are many ways of telling stories. Some people use words; some use lines and curves and colors, as in cartoons or pictures; and some use music.

It is not possible to separate the music and story in an opera. The composer always selects his libretto or story first and then composes music which can express the action and set forth the characters in the best manner possible. Of course the composer's feelings about the events and people are very important in his composition of the music.

In the earlier ballet, even though the dance is used to picture the story, much is left to the imagination of the audience, and there is not the close connection between the story and the music which is found in the opera.

But in many modern ballets, such as those created by the Russian Ballet of Diaghilev (dyä-gēē'lĕf), the music has been written with great care to fit and illustrate the action and the characters of the story.

Another kind of music which is connected with stories or plays, even though it may have neither song nor dance, is called "incidental music."

Scherzo from *A Midsummer Night's Dream* [V. R. G 560 B

FELIX MENDELSSOHN-BARTHOLDY (1809–1847), German composer. *Living in America at the same time:* ABRAHAM LINCOLN.

One summer day in Hamburg, a young fellow of seventeen was reading Shakespeare. He had picked up a German book which contained the comedy *A Midsummer Night's Dream.* Being somewhat sensitive, he was delighted by the delicate grace and humor which Shakespeare expressed in his poetry.

Over hill, over dale,
Thorough bush, thorough brier,
Over park, over pale,
Thorough flood, thorough fire,
I do wander everywhere,
Swifter than the moonë's sphere;
And I serve the Fairy Queen,
To dew her orbs upon the green.
The cowslips tall her pensioners be:
In their gold coats spots you see;
Those be rubies, fairy favours,
In those freckles live their savours;
I must go seek some dewdrops here,
And hang a pearl in every cowslip's ear.

Tunes started to race through this young man's head. He went to the piano. Soon the "Overture" to *A Midsummer Night's Dream* began to take shape. In a month it was finished. The music was full of youth, with a quaint mischievous gaiety. The young man was Felix Mendelssohn-Bartholdy (mĕn'dĕl-sōn bär-tôl'dĭ) (usually spoken of simply as "Mendelssohn"), who later was to become known as one of the great composers.

Many years later, in 1843, Frederick William IV of Prussia wished Mendelssohn to compose music for some plays, among which was the comedy by William Shakespeare called *A Midsummer Night's Dream.* So the composer added twelve other numbers to the "Overture," and this "Scherzo" was one of them. In spite of the fact that Mendelssohn was a grown-up man when he wrote it, the "Scherzo" seems to have as much sparkle and freshness as his earlier composition.

MEANING OF THE TITLE

Mendelssohn never wrote an opera, but his music for Shakespeare's *A Midsummer Night's Dream* entitles him to a place among the composers of dramatic music.

This is called "incidental music," which means that it is to be performed in connection with a play, to add to the action, to suggest an appropriate background of mood or feeling, or merely to make it more attractive. But Mendelssohn's music does not present in complete form the play which Shakespeare wrote. It is like program music* in that it expresses the mood and spirit of the various scenes in an imaginary way. It may be compared to a picture of great loveliness that represents a scene of delight and charm. Because of this, some knowledge of the play itself is likely to increase our enjoyment of the music.

THE STORY OF THE PLAY

The scene is set in and near Athens. The action centers about the gay preparations for the wedding of Theseus (thē′sūs), duke of Athens, and Hippolyta (hĭ-pŏl′ĭ-tȧ), queen of the Amazons.

The workmen of Athens are to perform a play to entertain the royal pair, and the rehearsal, which takes place in the woods near the city, is most amusing. For there are other people in the woods; two pairs of quarreling lovers and one pair of quarreling fairies, Titania (tĭ-tā′nĭ-ȧ), queen of the fairies, and Oberon (ō′bẽr-ŏn), their king. One of his followers is Puck, who is a clever sprite, or fairy, full of tricks and mischief. Oberon suggests that Puck turn his attention to teasing and fooling Titania, as well as the two loving couples.

At length there comes an end to the confusion and quarrels, and all are happy again. Once more the scene is in Athens. The workmen perform their play before the duke and his royal bride, and the fairies steal in to bless the happy pair.

THE MUSIC

Often composers use musical terms as titles for their compositions. The word *scherzo* really means "a joke" or "a jest" and is often given to musical compositions that have a playful or merry mood. Usually such pieces are lively and gay, or clever and mischievous.

This "Scherzo" comes between the first and second acts of the Shakespearean comedy. It really is a prelude to Act II, which is all about the world of imagination where mischievous elves dart here and there, teasing everyone who crosses their paths.

The music moves so rapidly that one melody hardly seems to end before a new one enters. The composer wrote the term *allegro vivace* above the music. The performance not only is to be quick, but it must be lively as well.

The opening measures of the two melodies are given, to make it easier to follow the music as we listen. When we ride on a car or a bus and have to stand, it helps us to keep our balance if we can hold on to something, especially if the car is moving at a good rate of speed. This "Scherzo" goes along so quickly that we need the support of being able to see and *hold on* to the tunes as they hurry by. These two melodies are something which may help us in just the same way as the strap or metal bar.

FIRST MELODY

SECOND MELODY

It seems natural to think of certain instruments with music of this kind. Trombones and tubas are heavy and pompous in sound, and would be quite out of place. Mendelssohn uses the wood-wind and string choirs for the most part. Now and then we hear the horns and kettledrums, and if we listen carefully we may hear the trumpets.

The differences between soft and loud are very plain in this performance by Toscanini (tōs-kä-nē'nē) and the Philharmonic Symphony Orchestra of New York. With scarcely any change in the speed, the music moves on to a *pianissimo** finish.

On the score is this legend: "He goes? Who knows where the traveler goes?" The question remains unanswered, because this music belongs to the queer little folk who live in the land of imagination.

DESCRIPTIONS AND COMPARISONS

1. Describe the mood which is suggested by the first melody of the "Scherzo" from *A Midsummer Night's Dream.*

2. Can you suggest some other ideas with which this music might be used?

3. Suggest some musical terms of expression that could be used to describe the performance of this music.

4. Is there anything that especially appeals to you in Mendelssohn's use of the orchestra?

5. Would you say that this music describes something? Or does it simply give you an idea and allow you to furnish the details?

6. How much does the knowledge of the Shakespearean comedy add to your enjoyment of this music?

7. The tunes used by Humperdinck in his overture are more songlike than those used by Mendelssohn in his scherzo. How do you know this?

8. Is there any place in Humperdinck's opera where you think Mendelssohn's "Scherzo" could be used?

9. Which performance do you prefer?

10. Why?

11. It will help you if you will make a list of some words you have added to your vocabulary in connection with these two compositions. They will prove useful later on.

MENDELSSOHN THE MAN

A large number of composers have to make their way under great difficulties, but Mendelssohn grew up in a very happy home. His family was wealthy and their home was large and quite elaborate. His name "Felix," which means "happy," well describes his life. The big laughter-loving family was very fond of music, and the home in Berlin was the center for many social affairs and artistic activities. Young and clever people were coming in all the time for supper and staying on for gay evenings filled with music or informal plays.

Felix and his sister were both very gifted and were encouraged by their mother, who sat beside them as they practiced or played on the piano. The rules, however, were very strict, and the children began their studies at five o'clock in the morning. But all was not hardship for these children, since much pleasure was mixed with their work.

Many people think that anyone as fond of music as Mendelssohn could not be a real boy, but young Felix was. He was always eager for any kind of sport, he adored the water, had a keen liking for athletic games, and was an unusually good dancer.

On every other Sunday morning there were musical parties in the Mendelssohn dining-room, and a small orchestra furnished the program. It was not long before some of Felix's compositions were performed, and every famous musician who came through Berlin appeared sooner or later at the Mendelssohn "Sunday Mornings."

Needless to say, this experience helped young Felix in playing before audiences and in leading orchestras. In later years, when he went about on concert tours all the world welcomed him. In fact his whole life was full of joy, and his music reflects his sunny and happy disposition. His favorite motto was "Whatever is worth doing at all is worth doing well."

He had a great fondness for nature. One day, when he was entertaining some visitors, he said, "Now we will go to an open-air concert." They went out into the garden, where a nightingale was singing. "He sings here every evening," said Mendelssohn, "and I often come to listen and I sit in this corner if I wish to compose."

You may wonder why on page 61 his name is given as "Mendelssohn-Bartholdy." His father added the name Bartholdy when he and his wife, like some other members of their families, adopted Christianity.

PROGRAM MUSIC

Mendelssohn had a special fondness for "program music"—music that attempts to paint a scene or tell a story. (He was, by the way, an excellent amateur painter of landscapes; and his letters show a decided literary gift.) The clue to the scene or action may usually be found in the title of a piece of program music. The event or picture may be real or imaginary. The music does not describe the act or scene; music cannot do that. But it can express similar moods or surround us with the same kinds of thought and feeling that the composer experienced when he imagined or witnessed the scenes that inspired the music.

The great Russian writer Tolstoi (tŏl-stoi′) said that the artist expresses "a feeling he has lived through." In this "Scherzo" Mendelssohn does not describe the different details of the play, but he has composed music through which we may imagine something of the feeling which was his when he read the play.

8

EXCURSIONS
INTO
GREAT
MUSIC

After listening to such compositions as the *Nutcracker Suite* or the scherzo from *A Midsummer Night's Dream* it seems unnecessary to have any further explanation of program music, such as is given on page 65. But since a large number of compositions belong to the group known as absolute music, a simple explanation of the expression will prove useful.

It is perfectly natural that, hearing as much music as we do, we should now and then come upon words whose meaning is not altogether clear. One of these words is *symphony.*

ABSOLUTE MUSIC

The symphony belongs to the type of compositions which are described as *absolute music.** Already we have discovered that a composition based on a story has more meaning for us and gives us more pleasure when we know the story. In such cases this information has served as a clue to aid our understanding of the music.

In absolute music in most instances there is no description in the title to help the listener. Compositions in this group need no story to explain them. They neither imitate nor represent anything but music. Absolute music is music which depends solely on its own beauty. As someone has cleverly described it, "It is music for music's sake."

This does not mean that the music needs to be heavy or difficult. In fact, many movements of symphonies are as merry and interesting as compositions which belong to the group called program music.

Allegretto from Symphony No. 8 [V. R. G 541 A

Ludwig van Beethoven (1770–1827), German composer. *Living in America at the same time:* James Monroe.

This music is the second movement of Symphony No. 8 by Beethoven (bā'tō-vĕn).

Beethoven had a habit of composing his symphonies in pairs, a serious work followed by one in lighter mood. In 1812, just before the United States had decided to declare war on England, he finished his seventh symphony. This work is serious and full of deep meaning. So it seemed natural for him to turn his thought to something lighter and more playful.

After finishing his seventh symphony, Beethoven was not very well, and his doctor ordered him to go away for a rest. Just before he left, his friends gave him a farewell dinner, and among the guests was Johann Mälzel (mělt′zěl), the inventor of the metronome.* Beethoven, who was fond of fun, composed a little round,* or canon,* in honor of Mälzel, and all the group sang it. Beethoven joined in with them, singing soprano. We can imagine him in a light blue coat and white waistcoat, his face and eyes shining as he sang "Ta ta, Mälzel, farewell, farewell." This melodic phrase later was to be used in a comical take-off on the rhythmic, steady beat of the metronome, and the jolly little tune of the round became the main theme for the second movement of his Symphony No. 8.

THE MUSIC

This is the shortest movement in all the symphonies by Beethoven, and one of the most charming and graceful. The music is merry and playful, and there is also a good share of energy and action. In fact, the entire symphony is in a light mood and has something of the carefree, jolly quality we find in the merry tunes of Haydn (hī′d′n). Haydn (page 70) was Beethoven's teacher at one time, and may have had an influence on the serious, thoughtful young man.

The expression mark at the beginning is *Allegretto scherzando,** and as we listen to the music it is easy to see why Beethoven used it.

The movement opens with the theme of the round* which was sung by the group at the farewell dinner.

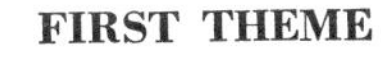

FIRST THEME

Underneath this melody (which is played by strings) there is an accompaniment by wood winds, playing in semistaccato* style some chords which suggest the ticking of the metronome.

It is interesting that the appearance on paper of the theme in sixteenth and thirty-second notes naturally makes one think that the music moves very rapidly. But the tempo indication is merely *Allegretto,** and conductors of orchestras realize that if the music is played too fast, the effect which Beethoven intended will be completely destroyed. So the speed is not as great as might be expected.

The second theme seems stronger and a little heavier than the first.

SECOND THEME

The accompaniment keeps repeating the chords, as if unable to stop. For variety Beethoven brings in the low strings with a smooth melody, and the movement ends with a quickening of the tempo that gives a feeling of merry humor and leaves us in good spirits.

THE DESIGN

We understand the meaning of *design* when it refers to the pattern of some fabric or the decoration of some familiar object of art. In music, too, the selection of the figure* and pattern is important, for they must be capable of being used in many ways if the design as a whole is to be interesting.

Quite often the design is made up of many repetitions of some special figure, and often composers in their writing introduce such a figure, which runs through the entire composition like a small repeated pattern in a tapestry or an Oriental rug. When we were learning about "Pomp and Circumstance No. 4," we found that such a figure was sometimes called a musical motto.*

In the second movement of his Symphony No. 8, Beethoven uses a three-note figure which comes at the beginning of the first theme:

FIGURE A

This tiny pattern is heard first at one pitch, then at another; played now by one instrument, now by another. It seems as if it were skipping about all the time. It is easy to recognize by its rhythm, if not by its tune.

In the middle section it seems to disappear for a moment, then back it comes with all the cheery confidence of the greeting "Here I am again."

THE SYMPHONY

When people plan a concert program they usually choose some music that is lively, some that is quiet; perhaps something jolly and something rather sad. In looking over programs we find that often they are divided into sections. One section will be merry and full of life, the next one peaceful and so on. The reason for using these different kinds of music is to increase, through variety, the interest and pleasure of the audience.

Do you remember how the suite was planned?

Symphonies are put together in the same way. It may be a good idea to know what a symphony is and to understand a few things about it.

1. A symphony is a large musical composition usually divided into parts, which may be compared to chapters in a book. These are called *movements*. Symphonies may have any number of movements, but most symphonies have four.

2. Any one of the movements may be played by itself, but all the movements are necessary to complete the plan of an entire symphony.

3. Although the form may require many different groups of instrumental players, a symphony is usually played by a large orchestra fully provided with strings, wood wind, brass, and percussion. Such an organization is therefore usually known as a *symphony orchestra*.

4. Some composers use numbers as titles of their symphonies, some use names of keys, and still others select a special name, such as "From the New World" (by Dvořák (dvôr′zhäk)), "Italian" (by Mendelssohn), or "Classical" (by Prokofieff (prō-kō′fē-ĕf)).

DISCUSSION

1. After listening to the music, do you feel that a movement from a symphony can be as enjoyable as a piece of program music?

2. With your knowledge of the incidents which have to do with this composition, do you think Beethoven has used the orchestra with good effect?

3. Is a knowledge of the form (page 74) necessary to interest in this music?

4. Why not make a list of the things in this music which interest you especially?

BEETHOVEN THE MAN

Probably the name of no other composer is so well known to people everywhere as Beethoven's. His childhood was similar to that of many of our great men. His family was very poor; and when Beethoven was still quite young, his father, knowing of the great success of Mozart, saw in his son's musical ability a probable source of support. So the child was forced to go through long hours of practice in order to develop skill as rapidly as possible.

He played the violin, organ, clavichord,* and harpsichord,* and even as a child showed the thoughtfulness which is found in most of his compositions. While he was still a youthful musician the newly invented pianoforte* took the place of the harpsichord and the clavichord. It was a fine instrument for Beethoven, because, as its name indicates, it could be played very loudly or very softly, as well as with many different shades of dynamics* between those two extremes.

He was not a very good businessman. In fact, he was always having difficulty with his landlords and sometimes moved so often that he didn't even bother to have his piano set up on legs but sat on the floor when he played it.

Deafness overtook him in early manhood and was a great source of unhappiness to him. Picture for yourself the tragedy of not being able to hear, and what it must have meant to Beethoven, the musical genius, who had always been able to hear much better than the average person. He wrote to some of his close friends that the hardship caused him the least trouble in playing and composing, and the most trouble in his association with people, as he couldn't tell what they were saying.

However, the misfortune of Beethoven's deafness resulted in a real gain for music. Because he could no longer hear himself play, he gave all of his time and interest to composition and, for the most part, wrote for the full orchestra.

His music expressed his own inner strength of character, his disposition, and his original ability, and he was free from any desire to show off with a display of skill in a brilliant performance. He gave us some of the most wonderful music that has ever been written, and because of it the name and works of Beethoven will always be a powerful and living influence in the world of music.

BEETHOVEN'S TEACHER

Thirty-eight years before Beethoven was born, a little boy who was to have a great influence on the development and progress of music was born in a small Croatian (krō-ā'shĭ-ȧn) village southeast of Vienna. His name was Franz Joseph Haydn. His father was a carriage-maker and his mother a cook in the household of a count. She used to sing the folk songs of the Croatians while his father accompanied her on the harp. Haydn would sit near by, pretending to play the violin with two pieces of wood.

One day a cousin saw him doing this and offered to take the boy home with him and teach him music. So, when only six years old, Haydn began to practice and study, learning something of the instruments most commonly used, and also receiving some voice training. He was worried.

though, because he could not keep himself neat and spotless, and so took to wearing a wig "for cleanliness."

One day the organist and choirmaster of St. Stephen's Cathedral in Vienna made a visit to the small village and heard Haydn's voice. He was so pleased with the sweet tone quality of it that he took the boy back with him to sing in the great cathedral. Soon he began to cover every piece of music paper he could lay hands on with his compositions. Young Franz lived in a house with the other choirboys and was full of mischief and pranks. One day he cut the pigtail off a schoolfellow. For this he was whipped and sent away.

Again we see him, in an attic room, playing on a little "worm-eaten clavier,*" writing music, practising his violin, teaching, and turning his hand to any musical experience that offered itself.

But his luck was to change. An Austrian nobleman named Esterhazy (ĕs′tẽr-hä-zē) invited Haydn to his home to write music for his private orchestra. This was a common practice in those days. Mozart, Purcell, and many other composers were hired by noblemen to compose music for them and for their friends. Almost all the large estates and country houses had bands or orchestras to entertain the family and friends of the owner. From now on this was to be Haydn's life, and a happy one it was.

For thirty years he lived at the beautiful castle of Prince Esterhazy, where there were wonderful theaters, summerhouses, deep parks, and a fine band of singers and players. Most of Haydn's compositions for voice and orchestra were written at Esterhàz.

It is interesting to remember that Haydn was the teacher not only of Beethoven but also of Mozart.

Minuet from Symphony No. 13, in G Major [V. R. G 560 A

FRANZ JOSEPH HAYDN (1732–1809), Austrian composer. *Living in America at the same time:* GEORGE WASHINGTON.

MINUET

On page 37 we found, in reading about the "German Dances" by Mozart, that the minuet was a favorite dance of the court in Vienna in the eighteenth century. It came from France, and because the manners and habits of those times were full of pomp and ceremony it is not surprising to find dignity reflected in the music of the dance. Although the minuet is like a waltz, it is much slower, for the leisurely steps of the dancers were mixed with graceful bows and curtsies.

Later the word *minuet* was used as the title of a musical form known as three-part song form with trio.* It was common practice for the early writers to use this form as the third movement of their symphonies. Although in early times the minuets in the symphonies were played just as rapidly as today, dance minuets were played more slowly and were quite dignified and stately.

THE MUSIC

Without any introduction, the flutes and violins give out the rhythmic and cheerful music of the first theme.

FIRST THEME

This theme is divided into two phrases,* the second phrase being two measures longer than the first.

The first theme is repeated, and then we hear another theme which resembles the first very closely.

SECOND THEME

The second theme continues with the same energy which is heard in the first theme and leads into a restatement of the opening phrase from the first theme. Then all the music, beginning with the entrance of the second theme, is repeated.

Up to this point the music seems to be divided into two fairly large and well-marked sections. The first centers around the opening, or first, theme, while the second section contains music from both themes.

These two sections make up the first division, or Part A, of the " Minuet."

THE TRIO

The second division of a minuet, Part B, is commonly called the *trio*. Almost everyone who has heard a brass band play a march knows what a trio is. The reason for the name is that long ago, in writing instrumental pieces such as the march, gavotte, minuet, and other dances, composers wished this second division, or Part B, to be different from Part A, for the sake of contrast. If Part B was lyric or quiet like a song, then Part A might be more lively and dramatic. So they wrote the second division in three-part harmony for performance by an instrumental trio.* Although the three-part harmony has been set aside, the name *trio* still is used.

The Trio opens with the following theme:

THIRD THEME

After this theme is repeated, a new theme — the fourth in the "Minuet" — is heard:

FOURTH THEME

It is quite similar to the third theme — the first theme of the Trio.

1. What is the most noticeable difference between these two melodies?
2. Is the difference one of style?

A repetition of the fourth theme brings the Trio, or Part B, to a close.

In the Trio the accompanying instruments support the melodies with smooth harmonies which are quite simple. The low strings do not move about as in Part A, but maintain a single interval (two tones a certain distance apart) for each phrase of four measures. This produces an effect which is called a *drone bass*.*

In "German Dance" No. 6, the one called "The Organ-Grinder," by Mozart, there was an illustration of *pedal point*,* which gives a similar effect.

After the trio section, the first division, Part A, returns, but this time neither of its sections is repeated.

Can you make a diagram which will serve as a plan of the form of this minuet?

If you answer these questions it will help you to make such a diagram.

1. How many sections are there in this movement?
2. Are any of these sections similar in feeling?
3. How many themes are there in each section?

THE FORM

However beautiful tones may be in themselves, they cannot give pleasure if they are sounded at random. They must proceed in gracefully ordered fashion. The study of the form of a composition is valuable only when it aids us in understanding the music better in order that we may receive a greater amount of enjoyment when we hear it. Form in music is very much like form in anything else. Any composer who intends to express a musical idea arranges his materials—rhythm, melody, and harmony—in such a way that they may express his idea clearly and that the listeners may understand his meaning. If we are able to recognize some of the parts of this organized plan, such as repetitions and contrasts, we will discover some features of beauty in the music which otherwise might remain unnoticed.

1. As you listen to the music, do you think the Trio provides enough contrast, both in musical feeling and in the style of performance?
2. Would this "Minuet" be good for dancing?
3. Are there any important features of this music that have **not** been present in some other selections to which you have listened?

THE ORCHESTRA OF HAYDN'S TIME

Orchestras in the time of Haydn were similar in size to most of the orchestras which we have now, although they did not have all of the wind instruments which are found in the orchestras of today.

In Paris many rich and fashionable people in society supported a series of concerts. Haydn composed this symphony for one of these programs. The audience at these concerts included lords and ladies of the court, as well as other leaders of society. Marie Antoinette is known to have attended many of them. The brilliant dress of the audience was matched by that of the members of the orchestra, who wore satin coats with gold and silver embroidery, hats with plumes, swords, and lace ruffles on their sleeves. These often interfered with the skill of their performance, especially in the case of the players of stringed instruments. These concerts were the more remarkable when we realize that at this time the people of our country had not elected their first President. In fact the symphony in which this minuet occurs was composed in 1787, the very year that the constitutional convention was trying to form the government of our country.

The fashionable concerts for which this music was written did not continue for long, however, for after two years the French people had their great Revolution, with the fall of the Bastille (bȧs-tēl′) and the ruin of the wealthy nobility, who had been the chief patrons of music.

Galloway

"Big Ben," in the Parliament Buildings, London, Is Famous the World Over

Galloway

No Visitor to London Ever Wants to Miss the Colorful "Changing of the Guard" at Buckingham Palace

Because this music was composed in the same year as the "German Dances" by Mozart (page 37), it may be interesting to hear these dances again and to compare them with this minuet by Haydn.

1. Do you think that Haydn's music is like Mozart's "German Dances"?
2. If so, in what respects?
3. Can you, in a few words, point out any way in which the music of Haydn and Beethoven is alike, as you have noticed it in these two movements of their symphonies?
4. Does the study of the form of one composition help you to understand form in other music?
5. How?

SIGHT-SEEING THROUGH MUSIC

ALTHOUGH he was not born in London, Eric Coates went there as a young student. He has written of those early days of struggle, when he was so poor that he had to trudge through city streets without any money either for bus rides or for a hot meal.

As a youth he learned all the interesting spots in this great city of the old world. Now, as a man, he writes, "I love London and nearly everything in it. As I write this, I am sitting in the living room of my flat, which is on the top floor of one of the highest blocks of flats in London.

"The room is light and airy and the sun pours in all day. I hear the distant sounds of traffic on one side of me, and see the green open spaces of the park on the other side. I am so near the hurry and bustle of busy life, yet so far away from it. In fact, all is very peaceful and quiet within my home."

London Suite [V. R. 36129 A, B; G 525 A

ERIC COATES (1886–), English composer.

MUSIC OF THE SUITE

Evidently he wanted other people to visit this English city and share his love and enthusiasm for it, for he composed the *London Suite,* in three movements, to describe it in sound and rhythm. To each number he has given a title which represents some spot that all visitors should see. These titles are:

1. Covent Garden 2. Westminster 3. Knightsbridge

Although each of these numbers is a complete selection, it is quite necessary that we hear them all, one after the other, so that the impression of London which we receive from the music may not be one-sided.

1. COVENT GARDEN

Covent Garden is the name not only of a famous old London opera house but also of the great vegetable and fruit market in which it stands. In his music Eric Coates takes us on an early morning excursion to the market. There is the usual clatter and the hurry and scurry that seem as much a part of a great market as the produce itself.

Some bright chords inform us that our trip has begun. The composer says that this music is a *tarantella,* which is a lively and exciting dance of Taranto (tä′rän-tō), in the south of Italy; the first melody has all the spirit and life of such a dance.

The second melody also is important. It is more singable than the first, but none the less energetic.

All the instruments in the orchestra have a share in playing these two melodies, and a feeling of gaiety is added by some countermelodies* played by the wood winds. The first melody alternates, or takes turns, with the second. It is heard first in the high register,* then in the low. The two themes move through different tonalities,* or keys,* until finally a new melody is heard.

There are certain customs that began years ago that have been passed on from one generation to another, and such an important thing as the market has many traditions and customs. To remind us of these practices which continue strong through the years, the composer has used the familiar melody of an old English song, "Cherry Ripe." This is the first part of the tune of this song as the people have sung it for many years:

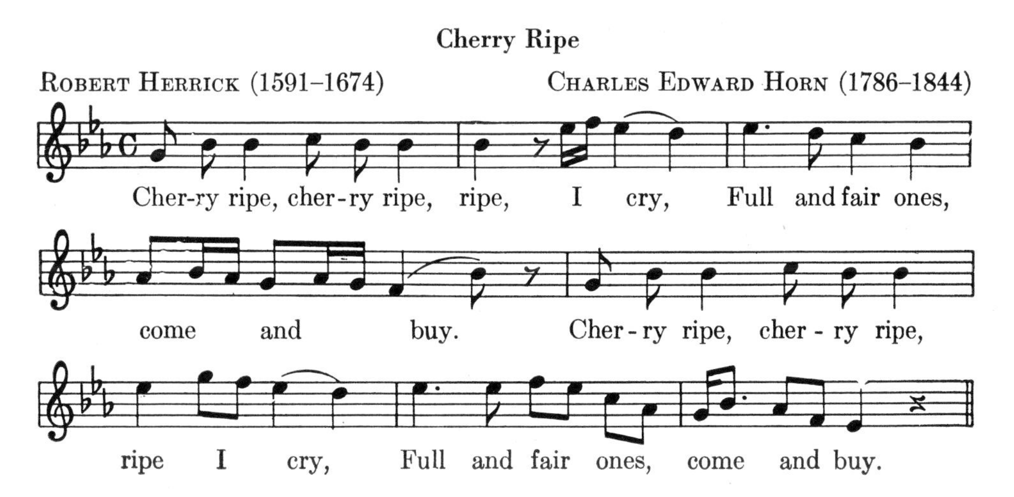

In the *London Suite* this melody is taken by the horns and low wood winds, with an accompaniment by the harp.

THIRD MELODY

At last the violins are heard playing this familiar tune. But only for a short time. Suddenly the first melody breaks in on this English melody, which is a reminder of days gone by. Once more we are in the bustle and hustle of the market. "Cherry Ripe," as though unwilling to go, returns, and this time it is livelier and brighter than before.

The drums beat out in steady rhythm

Then everything seems to slow down, and with heavy accents the first measures of the first melody are heard again. But the composer seems to say, "Presto, change!" and our visit to Covent Garden ends in a whirl of rapid notes and rousing chords.

2. WESTMINSTER

"Meditation" is used as a second title for this movement. The calm of Westminster Abbey, a spot which has occupied a prominent place in English history, is felt immediately, for the introduction begins with slow-moving chords played by strings and harp. The composer leads us on a leisurely tour of this ancient cathedral by the river, and the cellos play the opening melody with smooth tones against an accompaniment which sounds like chords on the organ.

FIRST MELODY

The time* changes, and the violins and oboes play a new melody that moves more rapidly. It seems as though the spell of the dream were interrupted with memories of some happy and even gay experience.

SECOND MELODY

The melody moves on to a strong climax, and then the first melody with which the movement opened is brought back by the strings. As this composition closes, the world-famous chimes of "Big Ben" are heard.

3. KNIGHTSBRIDGE

Knightsbridge is the name of a street that runs along the southern edge of Hyde Park, near Buckingham Palace. It has also come to mean a section of London between that thoroughfare and the Palace. One of the special attractions of this section which draws the attention of visitors is the soldiers of the Palace guard, with their tall black busbies (page 8) and red coats.

Eric Coates has given us a picture of these stalwart Englishmen as they parade or take part in the "changing of the guard," while moving and restless crowds of admirers watch the spectacle.

There is an interesting incident connected with the music of this third movement. The Suite had been published about a year and was selling in a quiet, steady way when, quite by chance, the third movement, the "Knightsbridge" march, was chosen as the "signature" for "In Town To-night," one of the popular radio programs of the British Broadcasting Company.

This spirited music took the English world by storm. The curiosity of the public was immediately aroused, and within a very few weeks thousands of letters poured into the radio studio asking for the name of the popular "signature" tune. The composer was swamped with requests to "appear in person" at every kind of entertainment and in all manner of places.

The introduction to the third number of the Suite not only shows us that this is a march but also contains the melodic figure which occurs in the first two measures of the first melody. Probably one reason for the popularity of the movement can be found in the first melody, which is full of energy.

FIRST MELODY

Does this tune seem to be anything like the first melody in "Pomp and Circumstance No. 4"?

This melody is played by first violins and oboe against a well-accented, but not too loud, accompaniment played by the full orchestra.

A second melody follows. This is shorter than the first, and leads right back to the opening measures of the first melody.

SECOND MELODY

These two melodies make up one division or section of this third movement of the *London Suite.*

The trumpets and horns make their appearance with a familiar musical figure which moves like this:

They are answered by the strings with this theme:

This musical conversation continues, the harmony changing and the volume increasing, until we hear a new tune played by the violin and cello.

THIRD MELODY

This is repeated, and in the repetition there are slight changes in the closing measures.

The first and second melodies are heard again and are just the same as in the beginning. The conversation between the brasses and strings is also repeated and once more the third melody is heard, this time in a different key. The presence of all the strings and the higher pitch* of the new key make the effect very much brighter than when this melody was heard at first.

After a rousing climax the first melody returns and moves into a coda. At a slower tempo and as if in triumph the third melody is heard once more, and the movement and the suite close with pomp and dignity. To anyone who has ever had an opportunity to visit Knightsbridge this music expresses the thrill, the movements of the crowd, and even the pageantry of the soldiers.

The Rondo

What about the form of the music of this movement? It can be easily explained. We have already noticed that the first division had two melodies and that the first melody was repeated. The form of this division may be represented by A B A.

The third, or C, melody is introduced by the brasses in a brilliant series of chords and it is heard twice. The letter marking of this second division of the music, therefore, is *Introduction* C C.

The first division now returns, and then the second division is repeated.

The opening melody, followed by a coda, completes this "Knightsbridge" march. Using letters only, we find that the order of melodies is as follows (it is not necessary to mention the repetition of C):

A B A C A B A C A

The name given to such an arrangement of melodies is *rondo*, for the music of the first section keeps "coming *around*" after each new section. The two outstanding qualities of the rondo, as of every other effective form, are *unity* and *variety* (page 32). The unity is brought about by the constant repetition of the first, or A, melody; variety is provided by the introduction of new melodies. It is not necessary that the first melody should always remain exactly the same in its repetitions. It may be changed slightly either in rhythm, in harmony, in key, or in pitch, or some form of decoration may be added. But the rondo itself (this does not include the coda) must end with the same melody with which it began, and there must be more than two melodies.

DISCUSSION

1. After hearing the music and reading this explanation, can you make up your own definition of *rondo*?

2. Can you tell what the difference is between rondo form and song form?

3. Can you draw a design for this piece of music, using curves, crosses, straight lines, or any other pattern which will illustrate the differences between the different melodies?

4. Are there any two movements of the *London Suite* that are alike in any way?

Probably you have never heard any music by Eric Coates before.

1. After hearing this Suite, can you list any qualities in his music which make his compositions popular?

2. How does this Suite differ from those you have heard already?

3. How does it compare with them in (*a*) the appeal of the music? (*b*) the interest of the story? (*c*) the use of instruments?

4. Could this Suite have the title of some other city than London and still be suitable? (Please be definite in your answers.)

5. Is the title necessary to enjoyment of this music?

SOMETHING ABOUT THE COMPOSER

Quite often it is easier to learn about the life and work of a man who lived long ago than it is about one who is alive today.

Eric Coates, who has given us these tonal pictures of everyday life in London, is the son of a country doctor. He was born in the county of Nottinghamshire, which, you may remember, was Robin Hood's country. He says of himself, "Music seems to have been in my life from the beginning, and my earliest memories are of lying awake in bed, listening to my mother as she played and sang in the parlor below."

As these were the days before radio, everyone who could play an instrument or sing was pressed into service, and twice a week the family orchestra (anyone who wished might join) met for rehearsals. Young Eric played both violin and viola, and he believes that it was in this group that he received his first desire to be a composer.

It took a good deal of arguing and pleading before his father consented to let him try his hand at music as an occupation. But finally it was decided that he should study at the Royal Academy of Music, in London, for a year. So "off I went," he writes, "and how glad and proud I was to be a student at that great training college."

After the first year it was agreed that he should "keep himself" and this meant harder work, as well as going without many things. Small jobs, such as playing in theater orchestras, and now and then performances and publication of his own compositions, helped him to increase his income. His present success is due to his determination as well as to his musical ability.

And then, after he had left his student days behind, a seemingly chance meeting changed the plan of his life. He describes it in this way:

> I decided to go to a concert by the Academy students. The concert was dull and I was bored — so bored, I was thinking of getting up and going home; when suddenly my whole attention became fastened on a student who had walked on to the platform to recite. She was very young, — sixteen to be exact, — and slim and fair.
>
> It is curious how quickly we change. I forgot about going home. I forgot that I was bored. I forgot everything but the girl on the platform. So that is how I first saw the lady who later did me the honor of becoming my wife, and who has helped me so much in all my work.

Eric Coates has sometimes been called the "Melody Man" and the free and singable style of his writing shows how great a part melody plays in his work. Also, he has been determined to keep up with the times. He is very fond of dancing and so has made himself familiar with all kinds of dances. He does not hesitate to use these dance rhythms in his compositions and his work has aroused much interest on this account also.

Today he is the leader among English composers of light music. He says, "Be sincere in all that you do; and whether you are a composer of symphonies or a writer of the lighter kind of music, always give of your highest and best. Only work that is refined and finished well lasts through the years, and good workmanship always finds its reward in the long run."

10

MUSIC THAT IMITATES ITSELF

Most people who can sing at all, and maybe some who cannot, probably have joined with a group at some time or other in singing a round. It may have been "Three Blind Mice," "Little Tom Tinker," or "Frère Jacques." There is a lot of fun in watching for our turn to begin the tune and then carrying it on until only one voice remains to finish the performance.

Not every melody is made in such a way that it will sound well with itself when a second voice begins singing it after the first voice is well started. Here is a familiar melody, however, that works out pretty well. In a round the second voice sings exactly the same melody as the first voice, and so on with the other voices; but in this illustration the second voice, after the first two measures, does not imitate exactly the melody which the first voice sings.

One thing which makes it easy for us to understand this unusual arrangement of "Dixie" is that the tune is familiar. It is like some friend who surprises us one day by appearing in a new suit and hat. Although we recognize the person because the well-known features are there, still the appearance is different.

Robert McBride, an American composer, remembered a little tune which he, as well as many other boys, whistled when he was a lad. Then he decided on a way to fix it up so as to present it in a musical composition. It is refreshing to find a composer who is not afraid to put honest work into a humorous or witty idea. Even the greatest composers have sometimes amused themselves and us in this way.

Fugato on a Well-Known Theme [V. R. G 505 A

ROBERT GUYN MCBRIDE (1911-), American composer.

THE TITLE

The title indicates that Robert McBride chose the *fugato* (fōō-gä'tō) as the best form in which to develop his merry notion. A fugato is something like a round. The same melody enters in different voices.

The rules governing these voices and their various entrances (page 91) are not as strict as in a *fugue,** which is really the parent of the *fugato.* In fact the fugato form allows the composer quite a good deal of freedom. Even though the melody appears in different voices, it is not necessary to follow a fixed plan. It is no wonder, therefore, that the fugato appealed to Robert McBride because of the liberty this form offers.

THE TUNE AND WHAT IS DONE WITH IT

FIRST THEME

This fugato suggests that Robert McBride is a modern musical humorist. That is, he tells his jokes with tones and rhythms just as other people use words. It is amusing music, for there is a natural desire to smile as we recognize a familiar and lively theme in an unusual setting, and follow its various adventures.

It is a cleverly written piece, and while it takes only three minutes to play, in this short time it shows a startling variety of instrumental and melodic effects. One newspaper says of it: "Mr. McBride's music, that took some three minutes to play, had so much life, so much honest skill in instrumentation, so much contagious fun, that the audience wanted to hear the piece a second time."

When the first theme or principal melody is repeated, it is in a different key and the second theme is heard below it.

SECOND THEME

Then the second theme appears on top, while the first theme is played in the low strings. It is easier to follow the second theme in this passage. The instruments are very much like voices singing a "round," for the high wood winds play the first theme once more, and then we hear the second theme. It is played by the French horns this time, and the first theme is heard below it, played by the bassoon. From now on the second theme seems to disappear, and the composer concentrates his attention on the first theme.

Brasses, strings, oboe, clarinet, and piccolo are heard tossing this familiar tune (first theme) about. Sometimes it is in the original rhythmic pattern, and sometimes the time values of the notes are lengthened, giving an impression of boastful dignity. In the midst of all this excitement the rhythmic pattern of the first theme:

is heard in the strings and then in the percussion. Before anyone has a chance to think that the composer is continuing his musical fun too long, the brasses give out a strongly syncopated* rhythm, and the music vanishes.

DISCUSSION

When we are singing a song it is a simple matter to follow the movements of the principal melody. It is easy to listen to this fugato; and we have no difficulty in recognizing the entrances of the first theme, now high, now low, alone or in company with other instruments, because the tune is familiar to us. Even the first note, with its three grace notes,* , is enough for us to understand what is happening, and we can find much amusement in the movements of this funny little melody. It is easy also to compare it with the second theme and to notice the contrasts, as well as to discover the things which are alike in the two themes.

1. After listening to McBride's "Fugato," can you tell whether you have heard any other music like this before?
2. If it is true that the composer is a musical humorist, what musical means does he use to express his humor?
3. How does this music prove that Mr. McBride uses the orchestral instruments in a skillful manner?
4. What places in the music best justify the name "Fugato?"
5. Describe in your own way your ideas about this "Fugato on a Well-Known Theme," referring to the features which seem to you outstanding.

THE COMPOSER

Arizona, with its mountains and desert, palm trees and cacti, its skies of clear blue, and bright-colored rocks, these were the surroundings of Robert McBride's childhood. He was born in Tucson and educated there from primary school through college. While he was studying at the university, there was in the music department a small group of students who tried to express in original compositions their impressions of this Western state, and McBride was among their number.

He had been brought up among musical people, as his father was the organist of one of the Tucson churches.

Name some other composers who grew up in a musical family.

Robert played in dance orchestras in and about southern Arizona, shifting from saxophone to oboe, clarinet, piano, and other instruments. This practical experience provided him with an inside knowledge of the orchestra and its possibilities.

At present he is teaching music at Bennington College, Vermont, and his compositions prove his great skill in instrumentation and his originality in melodic invention.

FORM IN MUSIC

When we read a book or see a play, it is not necessary to know "what is going to happen next" every minute. Our interest depends upon whether there is a good plot or not. Daniel Gregory Mason says: "Form is to music what a plot is to a story. It is the order in which things happen."

In many ways a person who writes music does not work differently from the author of a story. The composer finds interesting and attractive melodies and these help him to decide on his plot or form; or he may start with the desire to write in a given form and find melodies to suit it. In fact, if the form is the plot, we may compare the melodies to characters in the story.

Realizing that no one enjoys a story whose meaning is not clear, but gets a great deal of pleasure when he is able to understand what is taking place, the composer tries to join his music materials in some design, or form, that not only has beauty, but is easy to comprehend.

For this reason it is desirable that everyone who listens to music should try to fix the most important melodies in his memory, so that he can recognize them when they reappear under different conditions. The satisfaction which comes from being able to recognize these melodies adds a great deal to the enjoyment of the music.

A FUGUE

Many people believe that in order to understand a fugue* a person must have a very keen mind. In fact it is considered by some as the most intellectual form of composition that there is. But it is not difficult to understand after we have had some experience with it. Also, when it is well played, music written in the style of a fugue can provide one of the most exciting of all musical experiences.

In the "Fugato" by McBride we have discovered the relationship between a fugue and a round. We have also found that it is most important to be able to recognize the principal theme, for this knowledge is a great help in following what is going on in music written in the style of a fugue.

The Cat's Fugue

[V. R. 1664 A

DOMENICO SCARLATTI (1685–1757), Italian composer. *Living in America at the same time:* ISRAEL PUTNAM.

THE TITLE

There is a rather interesting story about this music. Biographies tell us that Domenico Scarlatti (dō-mā′nē-kō skär-lät′tē) was very fond of his large black cat. In fact the cat is present in many pictures of the composer.

A German composer, Johann Hasse (yō′hän häs′ĕ) by name, was a pupil of Scarlatti in Naples. A small dog belonging to Hasse had a habit of teasing Scarlatti's cat, and once in fright the cat jumped onto the keys of the harpsichord* and raced up and down. Report has it that Scarlatti wrote down the tones played by the cat in his wild scramble and used them as the main idea for the theme of this fugue.

THE MUSIC

It is important to see and sing, if possible, the melodic subject,* or principal theme, of this fugue.

PRINCIPAL THEME

This is an unusual pattern for a theme. First the melody goes up as though leaping over two or three stairs at a time. Then it turns and comes running down. The difference in the rhythm of the first three measures and the rhythm of the rest of the melody makes it easier to discover the entrances of the theme. If you will tap the rhythm of the theme you will discover how true this is.

Although the key signature* is that of F major or D minor, the tonality* of the melody seems strange because of the chromatics* in the second and third measures.

If the "Cat's Fugue" were played by an orchestra, and different instruments played the melody when it appeared at one time or another, it might be easier to follow the movements of the theme than in this performance where there is but a single instrument and therefore much less variety in instrumental tone.

This fugue is one of Scarlatti's many compositions for the harpsichord, so it is only right that the "Cat's Fugue" should be played by Flora Stad (page 52) on the harpsichord instead of on the modern pianoforte, which is quite different in tone.

MATTERS TO THINK ABOUT

Scarlatti chose something quite difficult when he set out to write a fugue with such an unusual theme as this. It is not singable, and it has strange, awkward intervals.* Yet the composer has succeeded in producing not only a complete fugue, but one that is attractive and interesting as well.

If you are able to recognize the various entrances of the melodic subject of this fugue, you will find it easy to discover what else is happening when the theme is not heard so clearly.

1. As you listen to the music, can you tell when this theme enters and how many times you hear it?

2. Does it seem as though there were different voices, such as soprano, alto, tenor, and bass, which take turns in singing the theme?

McBride's "Fugato" was written very recently; the "Cat's Fugue" was composed about two hundred years ago.

Can you find any differences between these two compositions and describe them? (You should have musical reasons for your opinion.)

Some joker once described a fugue as "a composition in which there are several voices, and as the different voices come in one by one, the different people in the audience go out one by one."

After hearing the "Fugato on a Well-Known Theme" and the "Cat's Fugue" what would be your idea about this statement, and how would you explain a fugue?

SCARLATTI

Domenico Scarlatti lived at the same time as the great master composer of Germany, Johann Sebastian Bach, and George Frederick Handel (hăn'dĕl), the great Saxon musician who settled in England and whose "Messiah" is the best-loved oratorio all over the world.

Scarlatti was a true son of Naples, and the chattering, merry life of the streets of that city seems to speak in his music. Different rhythms, leaps, and runs, and all sorts of surprises are found in it.

In 1729 (the year Baltimore was settled, in Maryland) Scarlatti left Naples for Madrid, where he spent twenty-five years. Soon Spanish ideas found their way into his compositions, just as they did with Chabrier long years later (page 19). In his ears was the sound of Spanish guitars and clanging strings. As the harpsichord, with its plucked strings and light, tinkling tones, could produce guitar-like effects, Scarlatti often imitated these Spanish instruments.

His influence is seen in the works of many composers who followed him. He was the first to employ the practice of crossing hands when playing on keyboard instruments. In this way he produced entirely new effects.

COUNTERPOINT

Musicians use the word *counterpoint* to describe that kind of music where one melody is used to accompany another melody, or else itself. The exact meaning of counterpoint is "point against point" or "note against note." It is well to think of counterpoint as "melody against melody," or melodies running counter to each other. In the "Fugato on a Well-Known Theme" and the "Cat's Fugue" we have illustrations of counterpoint, or "contrapuntal writing," as it is sometimes called.

Sawders

While Robert McBride Creates Modern Music, Other Artists Are Creating Modern Cities

Loew's Inc.

The Dancers for Whom Johann Strauss Wrote His Waltzes

Some people feel that a fugue is such an involved kind of music that only very few can appreciate it. In fact they look on it as a sort of crossword puzzle for which they do not know the answers. This is a false notion of fugue. Music written in this form may be as beautiful, as moving, or as entertaining as that written in any other form; but it is true that too much attention to the details may destroy our enjoyment of the music. If we know the principal theme and think of the fugue as being sung by a group of voices, we can recognize the entrances of the subject, now in a high voice, then in a low, until all voices join in a grand performance which comes to a glorious climax.

Organ Fugue in G Minor [V. R. G 540 A

JOHANN SEBASTIAN BACH (1685–1750), German composer. *Living in America at the same time:* BENJAMIN FRANKLIN.

Bach (bäk) wrote this fugue for the organ, on which he was an expert performer. But on this record Olga Samaroff (ôl′gȧ sȧ-mä′rôff), an American musician, plays it on the piano. Such an arrangement for the piano of music originally written for other instruments is often called a piano *transcription** (page 105).

Bach wrote several organ fugues in G minor. This one is known as the "Little Fugue." One other, known as the "Great Fugue," will be presented later in this course.

THE MUSIC

One voice, the soprano, gives out the principal theme, or subject:

PRINCIPAL THEME OR SUBJECT

This is followed by three other statements, at varying pitches, of the theme. The alto begins this way, one *fourth* (that is, four notes of the diatonic* scale) lower:

Then the tenor voice is heard, just an octave* lower than the soprano, and finally the theme is heard in the bass, one octave lower than the alto.

As the bass finishes this theme we hear a more singable tune. This melody is important because it too occurs, either as a whole or in small parts, all through the composition.

COUNTERMELODY

As the music continues Bach changes both the mode,* from minor to major, and the key, and we hear the principal theme in B flat major.

After a passage in which both the principal theme and the countermelody are heard, weaving in and out, the composition works up to a strong climax, the bass giving out the principal theme with a great deal of energy, as if to make sure we do not forget it.

It is interesting to notice that the final cadence* of this organ fugue is in the major key of G. It was an old custom to let a musical composition in the minor mode end with a major chord; and this exchange of a minor third for a major third in the final chord was called the *Tierce de Picardie*, or the "Picardy Third." Many examples of it are found in Bach's music. The exact reason for the name is not known; but probably the custom was followed first in Picardy, in northern France.

DISCUSSION

In singing this principal theme you will notice that it begins with one-beat notes, but as the measures follow each other the rhythmic pattern becomes more elaborate, until in the final measure of the theme each beat has four notes. Although the tempo remains steady, there is an effect of more rapid movement.

1. Do you find it easy to discover the entrances of the subject theme in the different voices?

2. Do you think Bach has a direct and clear style of writing?

3. Do the melodic patterns and rhythmic phrases which move in counterpoint to the principal subject dim or blur the outline of the theme as it moves about in the various voices?

4. Of the three compositions "Fugato on a Well-Known Theme," "The Cat's Fugue," and this Organ Fugue in G minor, which is the easiest to follow? (Give musical reasons for your answer.)

5. Which do you like the best?

6. Why?

7. Do you think that the orchestra, harpsichord, and piano are satisfactory for the compositions which are performed by them?

JOHANN SEBASTIAN BACH

The Bach family had been musicians for over two hundred and fifty years. It was one of those large German families with aunts, uncles, and cousins. All of them could sing or play the harpsichord, organ, or violin. Family gatherings where original songs and instrumental pieces were performed were everyday matters for the Bachs.

Johann Sebastian, born in the year that the first fort was built on the site of the present city of Chicago, was even more gifted than others of his family in imagination, in thoughtfulness, and in a kind of inner joy.

Like so many of his family, he turned to the organ as his favorite instrument. When but a youth of fifteen he obtained a position in a choir, and at eighteen he took his first position as organist and began to write pieces for his favorite instrument.

Bach is always remembered in connection with the city of Leipsic (līp'-sĭk), where for many years he was cantor, or choir leader, of the Thomas School and organist of Saint Thomas's Church. This German city was the center for the great *Messen*, or fairs, which brought crowds of people to the city. In this way the fame of Bach as organist and composer was spread all through Germany.

During all the years when his duties of singing-teacher at the Thomas School secured him a living, Bach was busily writing chorales (a kind of hymn), and chorale preludes (elaborate organ pieces woven around the tunes of chorales); preludes, fugues, and suites for organ, clavichord, and harpsichord; and anthems.

His works had a wonderful singing quality. He would weave the voices in and out as another person would weave a basket. Each voice had a song of its own, and together they made harmony.

The ability to write counterpoint expressively was Bach's greatest gift. No other musician who has ever lived has been able to equal him in this kind of expression, and now in the twentieth century he is hailed as one of the greatest composers of all time.

11

THE ART SONG

A SONG PROGRAM

THE term *folk song* is usually associated with some country or race of people, while the term *art song* is connected with the name of some composer. All through our music experience in school we have been singing folk songs and art songs, even though the real difference between them may never have been explained. Many folk songs may be looked upon as art songs, because they have a charm and beauty which is similar to that found in the art song.

On page 13 under the heading "Music Pictures of Three Countries," a good deal was said about the value and importance of folk tunes, whether they are played or sung. *Art song* is a term used with a song in which a composer has given a desirable musical setting to a poem. In fact the poet and composer share the honors equally. An expression commonly used in connection with the art song is "thoroughly composed," because the meaning of each word or each phrase of the poem is reflected in the music.

In some art songs there is different music for each stanza. In others the same melody and accompaniment are used for all the stanzas; when this happens the art song is said to be *strophic** in style.

In writing art songs the composer wishes above everything else to have the melody express the meaning of the text and be as beautiful as possible. The accompaniment also must add to the artistic effect. Always there must be complete agreement between the text and the music.

"Lullaby" and "The Vain Suit" [V. R. G 510 B

JOHANNES BRAHMS (1833–1897), German composer. *Living in America at the same time:* JOHN HAY.

LULLABY

Nearly everyone is familiar with this cradle song, which begins as follows:

The poem was written by Karl Simrock and has been translated in many different ways. Here is one translation:

1

Lullaby and good night! to cheeks rosy bright,
To fingers safe hid 'neath coverlet white;
And again, if God will, shalt thou wake with the morn;
And again, if God will, shalt thou wake with the morn.

2

Lullaby and good night! till glad morning light,
While fairest of forms in dreams fill the sight;
And again, if God will, shalt thou wake with the morn;
And again, if God will, shalt thou wake with the morn.

Johannes Brahms (yō-hän'ĕs bräms) was a great lover of folk songs and collected them during his entire life. On some of his walks in the country he would stop along the way to listen to a mother singing to her child or perhaps to join a merry group on the village green.

At one time he was the leader of the Hamburg Ladies' Choir, and he made a practice of using many folk songs in its programs. This "Lullaby," or "Wiegenlied" (vē'gĕn-lēt), as it is called in German, is said to have its origin in one of the songs of this group.

But whatever its source, it probably is the best known and most generally loved of all Brahms's songs. The simple grace of the folk tune is found in this beautiful song which reveals Brahms's deep affection for children.

THE SONG

The rhythm of the cradle song is established in a two-measure introduction, and then the voice of Elisabeth Schumann is heard singing the familiar yet always appealing melody. The accompaniment is furnished by the piano.

Each stanza of the song is sung to the same melody. It may never have occurred to you when singing this song that there is little of variety in it. If the melody is divided into phrases,* each one having four measures, you may discover that Brahms used imitations and repetitions without being tiresome, and that the term *art song* is just as suitable to a simple composition like this as to something more elaborate.

1. After hearing this song can you suggest any special ways in which this song belongs to the group called art songs?
2. Does the interpretation by Elisabeth Schumann bring out these points more strongly than when you sing the song in a group performance?
3. Can you name any other songs that you have sung which are similar to "Lullaby" and may be called art songs?

THE VAIN SUIT

Another translation of this song gives it the title of "The Disappointed Serenader." These words "suit" and "serenader" are not very common; the first means a request, or plea; the second (as you would expect) means "one who is singing a serenade." In this song they refer to a love scene in which the serenader stands and shivers beneath the window of his sweetheart, but does not succeed in arousing her pity.

In this composition Brahms seems to be in quite a different mood from that in which he wrote the "Lullaby." Here there is a feeling of lightness and fun, and even a suggestion of teasing. The song opens with this melodic phrase:

The music seems to be having a good time with itself as it tells the troubles of the young serenader and advises him to go home and forget his difficulties, for time heals everything. Perhaps Brahms was laughing at himself as he composed the song, recalling some of his early romantic experiences.

Elisabeth Schumann sings the song in German, so you will need this translation to explain the humor which is found in the poem.

The Disappointed Serenader

1

HE. Fair maiden, good evening, good evening to you,
Right good evening to you.
For old acquaintance sake, an ounce of pity take,
Open wide your door,
Turn the key, slip the bolt,
Open wide your door!

2

SHE. Bolted fast is my door; I can let no one in,
I let no one in.
If I should open wide, mother would sharply chide,
She would chide me well.
She would frown, she would scold,
She would chide me well.

3

HE. So frosty the night and so cold is the wind,
So cold is the wind,
My heart will surely freeze; open, fair maiden, please!
Come and let me in.
Turn the key, slip the bolt,
Open wide your door.

4

SHE. Freeze, if you will, that poor, silly heart of yours!
That poor, silly heart of yours!
Come, hasten home to bed. Pillow your drowsy head!
Hasten home to bed!
Foolish boy, hasten home.
Good night, good night!

THE SONG

This song is like a conversation carried on by two people, and even without an accurate knowledge of the meaning of the text the changes in mood are easily discovered in the music. Notice, for example, how the mode changes from major to minor when the desperate lover begins to tell how cold the night is. Listen to the pianoforte accompaniment, which seems to imitate the sound of a wintry wind. Although Brahms never wrote an opera, his songs prove that he had rare ability in writing expressive and even dramatic music for voices.

Brahms's fondness for folk melody runs like a thread through all his compositions, for this song is said to come from the Lower Rhine. But the art and skill of the composer are very clear in its changes from the major to minor mode and in the important contribution of the instrumental accompaniment.

1. Is the accompaniment more necessary to the artistic effect of this song than in the "Lullaby"?
2. Can you give any satisfactory reasons for your opinion?

There are certain things in music which we think of as the materials with which a composer works in order to express his ideas in the best way possible. The most important of these materials are movement of the melodies, rhythmic patterns, and harmonic combinations. He organizes these according to some pattern, or form; chooses the suitable keys and the mode, either major or minor or (most often) both; and the result is a composition which shows the skill and ability of the man who wrote it.

1. Does Brahms seem to prefer one musical factor to another?
2. Can you suggest any special ways in which he deserves the name of a composer of art songs?

BRAHMS THE MAN

Pictures of Brahms show that he was a shaggy, bearlike man with a long beard and sea-blue eyes. Simple and unaffected, he had a great dislike for things that were false, but he loved everything fresh and true.

His father played the contrabass* in the theater orchestra in Hamburg, and there is a rumor that once, when a conductor told him that he was playing too loudly, the elder Brahms replied, "It is my own contrabass and I'll play it as loudly as I please."

It was very natural that Johannes Brahms should study music. He became an excellent pianist. When only twenty years old he went on a concert tour with a brilliant Hungarian violinist, and in this way came to know and love the gypsy rhythms and melodies. Robert Schumann (shōō'män), who at the time was a successful composer, as well as founder and editor of a famous musical magazine, and was twenty-three years older than Brahms, was the first to become enthusiastic over the talents of the young musician. He and his wife, Clara Schumann, took Brahms into their own group of friends, and he became famous overnight.

The young composer knew, however, that this was not real success. Wiser than his years, he chose to withdraw from the society of these eager musicians and give himself to years of study. He realized that the easy, romantic music suggested by a person's changeable feelings is not the highest kind of music. Feeling and thought must go together to produce art that is pure and noble.

When his symphonies finally appeared they were compositions over which the greatest pains and care had been taken. Every melody, as well as the form and instrumentation, had been worked over until each of these great works was expressive in its smallest detail and impressive and well rounded as an artistic whole.

Brahms is like the sculptor who, with high ideals and broad vision, molds and chisels until his work comes forth clear and beautiful.

"To the Nightingale" and "Lovers of Every Description"

[V. R. G 510 A

FRANZ SCHUBERT (1797–1828), Austrian composer. *Living in America at the same time:* ELI WHITNEY.

Some writers regard Franz Schubert as the father of the art song. Everyone recognizes that the music of many of his songs expresses the meaning of their poems quite as clearly as the words themselves. It seems as though he considered the poems for his songs as little librettos* and was constantly changing the music to fit the mood of the words.

Can you name any songs by Schubert which you know and enjoy?

The two songs by Franz Schubert in this program are not so familiar as some others. They are quite short and yet complete. The original titles and poems are in German; so it is desirable that the English translation be given. The poem for "To the Nightingale," by the German poet Matthias Claudius (klou′dĭ-o͝os), is translated as follows:

To the Nightingale

Now love within my breast lies sleeping,
By guardian angels lulled to rest,
By guardian angels lulled to rest.
With careless joy my heart is leaping,
And every leaf and blossom
A happy tryst with me is keeping.
Nightingale, pray, nightingale, pray,
Wake not his slumber today.

THE SONG

A short prelude* prepares the way for the song. Here are the first few measures of the melody:

It is not possible to listen to this song without noticing the importance of the accompaniment. Schubert believed that there were three very essential things to be considered in the composition of an art song:

1. A poem possessing real beauty.
2. A melody which follows the meaning and accent of the words without sacrificing musical feeling.
3. A harmonic background, or accompaniment, which will increase the artistic effect of the composition.

In this song, "To the Nightingale," he carries out his convictions. The short introduction prepares the hearer for the melody, which moves gracefully from the opening measures in the minor mode to a complete pause in the major key. There is a measure of interlude,* and the song continues with dainty melodic patterns and suitable harmonies. The last two lines of verse might, to the ordinary composer, seem to provide a satisfactory ending to the song, but not to Schubert. After the voice has stopped singing he adds a little postlude,* as though to call attention to the request expressed in the last line, "Wake not his slumber today."

1. Does the music alone give you any idea of the meaning of the text?
2. Do you think this melody is easy to understand?

LOVERS OF EVERY DESCRIPTION

Quite different is the second song on the record. The title gives the impression that the poem is not very serious, and the translation proves once again that all great composers and poets like to write about funny things once in a while. Schubert was very fond of the poems of Goethe (gû'tē), one of Germany's greatest poets, and chose many of them to set to music. This one, translated, reads as follows:

1

Were I a fish today,
So nimble and gay,
And you should come angling,
You'd soon find me dangling;
Were I a fish today,
So nimble and gay.

2

Were I a coin of gold
Your hand should enfold,
And you sought to spend me,
Away I would wend me!
Were I a coin of gold
Your hand should enfold.

3

But I am simply one
To take or to shun.
If better you're wishing,
You're free to go fishing;
For I am simply one
To take or to shun.

The poem suggests that Schubert might choose to set it in strophic style. And so he did. The melody is very simple and begins as follows:

1. After hearing this song can you describe the effect which is made by the little introduction?

2. Why do you suppose this introduction is used before each stanza?

3. Are there any other evidences of repetition besides the use of the same music for all stanzas?

4. Is there anything in the words that suggests that the melody ought to be simple?

5. Does the accompaniment add to the beauty of this song as it did to that of "To the Nightingale"?

A LITTLE ABOUT SCHUBERT

Imagine yourself entering a café in Vienna, some summer evening in the early 1800's. You have surprised a group of young men sitting about a table, singing noisily. Or perhaps they are shouting with laughter at some joke they have just played on one of their number.

In their midst you see a short, plump young man with curly hair and wearing spectacles. His stock (a kind of neckwear) is crumpled and twisted; his coat is shabby. While his companions are having a merry time, he is looking through a book of poetry, perhaps one by his fellow citizen, Goethe. His lips move as he says the lovely lines over to himself. Suddenly he begins scribbling on his cuff; or, seizing a menu card, draws a staff on the back and writes down a melody.

Of course this is Schubert occupied in song-writing. He was a great reader of poetry, and if a poem pleased him it set up musical echoes in his head. Even though he was very poor, his poverty did not stop him from making up beautiful melodies.

Schubert was turned out into the world to work and study when most other boys are protected at home. It was natural in those days for boys who were gifted musically to attend a school where choir singers were trained for the court chapel and where they received also a general education in music.

Together with many others Schubert went up to Vienna for a tryout. The group amused themselves over his queer gray suit, calling him a "miller," making fun of him, and telling all kinds of jokes. But when the examination took place, the joke was on them. Young Schubert outshone them all in his knowledge of music, and he soon changed the gray suit for the gold-laced uniform of a royal chorister, or choir singer, as he was called.

Almost the only time during his life when Schubert was sure of good food and comfort was when he became a music teacher in the household of Count Esterhazy. You will recall that you met his name when reading about Haydn (page 71). In the summer the Esterhazy family went to their estate in Hungary. From there Schubert wrote in his jolly way:

> The cook is a pleasant fellow; the ladies' maid is thirty; the housemaid is pretty; the nurse is somewhat ancient; the butler is my rival; the two grooms get on better with the horses than with us. The count is a little rough; the countess proud, but not without heart; the young ladies good children. I need not tell you, who know me so well, that with my natural frankness I am good friends with everybody.

Toward the end of his life Schubert became so poor that he once sold half a dozen of his beautiful songs for about ten cents apiece. It is easy to imagine that this hand-to-mouth existence, while he was burning up his energy in composition, did him much harm.

He was only thirty-one years old when he died, leaving over six hundred songs, besides compositions for orchestra, chorus, string quartets, and piano.

DISCUSSION

In the Song Program there have been two art songs by Brahms and two by Schubert.

1. Have you noticed any ways in which these composers seem to write alike?
2. Do you like one song better than any other?

The singer of art songs has an important responsibility.

1. Do you think that Elisabeth Schumann has sung these songs in a pleasing manner?
2. In what way?
3. Can soft tones give as much pleasure as loud?
4. Do you think that these songs are better for the soprano voice than for any other?
5. What are the different ways in which the music of the songs in this program has made the meaning of the words more interesting?

12

TWO MUSICAL SKETCHES FROM RUSSIA

WHEN we were listening to the *Nutcracker Suite* and talking about it, we learned that an American citizen of the same period as Tchaikovsky was Phillips Brooks, who earned the friendship of young and old alike through the words of the Christmas carol "O Little Town of Bethlehem." Tchaikovsky had the same ability to reach the hearts of people through his melodies as Phillips Brooks had through his words. Each man shows his love for those who lived around him in a simple yet beautiful expression that will never be forgotten.

The word "sketch" means the same thing in music as in art and literature — a short composition, simply constructed.

Can you name any musical selections with which the term "sketch" might be used?

In the title Tchaikovsky gives us an idea about the mood of this composition.

When composers do this, what kind of music do we call it?

Humoresque

[V. R. 1170 B

PETER ILYITCH TCHAIKOVSKY (1840–1893), Russian composer. *Living in America at the same time:* PHILLIPS BROOKS.

THE TITLE

The word "Humoresque" (hū′mĕr-ĕsk′) has been used by many composers as a title for any instrumental piece which is jolly and full of fun. One of the most familiar selections with this title was written by Dvořák (dvôr′-zhäk), a great Bohemian composer.

Do you remember this composition, and can you whistle or sing the opening measures?

Possibly it was because he had some French blood in his veins that Tchaikovsky always had a taste for French music. He was fond of the music of Delibes (page 27), and the opera *Carmen*, by Bizet (bē-zĕ′), was a great favorite of his. He visited Paris as often as possible for entertainment and recreation.

Can you suggest any particular things about Delibes and his music which might have appealed to this great Russian composer?

THE MUSIC

The melodies in this composition are more Russian than French, and the effect we get is of villagers having some kind of a local celebration. The melodies, and there are five of them, are odd and comic, and the music is full of brightness and good humor. There is no introduction; the piece opens immediately with a short tune that is almost querulous, or whining.

FIRST MELODY

This melody has been used in a motion picture to indicate a scolding busybody or village gossip. It is followed by this jolly little tune:

SECOND MELODY

The progress of this melodic passage seems to be interrupted, however, for a third melody is heard between the second melody and its repetition.

THIRD MELODY

Suddenly the feeling of the music changes. The new section is quieter. There is a gentleness about it that suggests green meadows or country hillsides. There are two different themes.

FOURTH MELODY

FIFTH MELODY

Then the dance returns, with the first three melodies; and the composition ends in what sounds like a scuffle and shuffle of feet as the dancers stop.

Can you mark the form of this composition by letters and give it a descriptive name?

The accompaniment for the most part is of no special interest and simply provides a harmonic background for the melody. But in the middle section the harmony has a little more variety, and little tunes and running passages add very much to the pleasing effect of the music.

THE PERFORMERS

No violinist has been more loved by American audiences than Fritz Kreisler (krīs′lẽr). He is almost as well known as a composer as he is as a performer. Although a native of Austria (he was born in Vienna), since he made his first tour of the United States (in 1889) he has been given a warm welcome whenever he returns. He has visited every civilized country in the world, making one triumph after another.

In this recording, as in his concert performances in this country, he is accompanied by Carl Lamson of Boston, Massachusetts. His ability as an accompanist is recognized everywhere, and he contributes very much to the enjoyment of Mr. Kreisler's performance.

Album Leaf

[V. R. 1170 A

Sergei Rachmaninov (1873–), Russian composer.

Although there was thirty years' difference in their ages, there was a very strong friendship between Tchaikovsky and Rachmaninov (räk-män′ĭ-nŏf). It happened like this: when he was only thirteen years old, Rachmaninov made a piano arrangement of one of Tchaikovsky's compositions and showed it to the great composer. From that time on the older man displayed a marked interest in the development of the young musician and helped him in many ways.

TRANSCRIPTIONS

On the printed score the title given is "Marguerite," with "Album Leaf" underneath. The title "Album Leaf" is sometimes given by composers to a little piece short and simple enough to have been written in a young lady's autograph album, as a poet might write a few lines of verse. It also says "Transcribed by Fritz Kreisler."

Fritz Kreisler has made transcriptions of many pieces by other composers. For example, the "Humoresque" was originally written for piano, but the music attracted Kreisler so much that he arranged it for violin solo with piano accompaniment. We have already found that the word "transcription" in music means a new arrangement of a composition for performance by a different instrument or group of instruments from that originally intended.

In some cases certain changes are necessary in order that the music in its new surroundings may sound as attractive and as lovely as in the original one. Thus a transcription in music may be compared to a translation in literature. Kreisler, in his transcriptions, often enriches the harmony and elaborates the accompaniment.

He has even confessed recently to having published as transcriptions a great number of pieces which were in reality original compositions of his own.

THE MUSIC

It is not difficult to follow a melody when it is played by a solo instrument with piano accompaniment, even though there may be many changes of key, little decorations may be added, and there may be no pauses to show when one tune ends and a new one begins. The reason for this is the difference in tone quality between the solo instrument and the one which accompanies it.

The opening phrase of this melody of "Album Leaf" is like a question.

FIRST MELODY

The tune moves along without interruption. There is a passage where it seems to wander through various keys without coming to any real stop, until the familiar notes of the introduction tell us that the opening phrase has returned.

This time, however, it is an octave higher than it was in the beginning. Now all the material which we have heard before is repeated with both melody and accompaniment in an upper register.* Of course this gives it a new meaning. The effect is tender and delicate, and probably this is one of the effects which Kreisler introduced in his transcription from the original.

There is a reminder of the opening phrase as the closing section begins. This section has a great many more runs and trills, as well as some dainty arpeggios* (är-pĕd′jō). The sketch comes to an end with soft chords.

In the Song Program we discovered that the singer had a responsibility when singing an art song, that of making the meaning of the song as clear as possible to the listener. The violinist has a similar responsibility.

1. As you recall the Song Program and listen to these Musical Sketches, do you think that the violinist's performance is as successful as the singer's?
2. Do these Musical Sketches sound to you like "songs without words"?
3. Can you suggest an idea for a poem that might be suitable for this composition by Rachmaninov?
4. What seems to you to be the chief attraction of this music?
5. Do you think it would sound well if it were played by an orchestra?
6. In your opinion, what is the reason for the violin's being such a favorite solo instrument?
7. Does either of these compositions have qualities that you think belong to Russian music?

SERGEI RACHMANINOV

This composer is known also as a remarkable pianist. For many years he has lived in the United States and makes concert tours playing his own works, as well as those of other composers. Rachmaninov's family was wealthy and owned an estate in the province of Novgorod (nôv′gō-rōt). Because his family was well-to-do, he never had to experience the poverty and hardship that surrounded some composers in their childhood.

Novgorod was in a very old part of Russia and was full of ancient traditions. In the early days this province was governed by its own princes, and it had its churches and monasteries when the rest of Russia was all upset. Rachmaninov grew up in the midst of this strong Russian feeling and his music is alive with it.

When he went to St. Petersburg (now Leningrad) he was a famous musician. Later he went to Moscow and fell under the influence of Tchaikovsky. We have read about this association and friendship on page 105.

In 1909 Rachmaninov came to this country. He was amused to find that the fame of his C-sharp-minor Prelude had come before him. You remember that is the pianoforte piece which begins with three solemn, descending chords, played slowly and with a good deal of force.

He is a serious composer, and a little thread of sorrow seems to run all through several of his compositions. This is natural, for inhabitants of the north country have a vein of tender sadness. His fame as a pianist is great and he can make the piano sound like a full organ.

13

RHYTHMIC MELODIES

We have already discovered that dance rhythms have always been favorites with composers, and that the waltz has been especially popular. In the program "Dances New and Old" (page 34) we found that the composer Richard Strauss used waltz rhythm in composing some very attractive music.

Can you recall any special musical qualities in the Waltzes from *Der Rosenkavalier*?

In comparing the music of any two composers it is helpful to know something about the circumstances under which the compositions were written, as well as any other interesting facts about the writers which may help us to understand the music better.

Probably you remember that Mozart was dance composer to the Viennese court and wrote many dances for different royal occasions.

THE WALTZ

Nearly one hundred years later, life was still gay in Vienna and as long as he lived Johann Strauss, otherwise known as the "Waltz King," produced his new waltzes at the Viennese court balls. These waltzes were eagerly awaited and received with great enthusiasm, the dancers stopping to applaud and the ladies throwing bouquets. These waltz tunes spread from the ballrooms to the gardens and theaters until they were whistled and sung by boys on the streets.

It was in Vienna that the waltz really became settled in the form in which we know it. There is an introduction, generally rather slow, which prepares us for the principal melody of the composition. Then several different waltzes, sometimes five or six, follow; and at the end there is a coda,* in which parts of the principal themes of the waltzes occur.

Tales from the Vienna Woods [V. R. 15425 B

Johann Strauss (1825–1899), Austrian composer. *Living in America at the same time:* Rutherford B. Hayes.

The Strauss family used to spend their summers outside the city, in the freshness of woods and fields. With their friends they enjoyed listening to music out under the trees, either sitting at tables or walking happily about. All that was needed to compose these waltzes, said Strauss, was a "happy thought. We often announced for a certain evening a new waltz of which, in the morning of the same day, not a single note had been written. In such a case the orchestra players went to the composer's home. As soon as the composer finished a part, it was copied and he dashed on to the next." This may account for the simple and delightful melodies which have made Strauss waltzes so popular.

THE MUSIC

There are five waltzes under the single title "Tales from the Vienna Woods." Some of them have two different melodies. In this arrangement the introduction contains the first melody of the second waltz.

Although it is not difficult to recognize the entrance of the different melodies as the music moves along, it may be helpful to follow these tunes in this book while the record is being played.

WALTZ NO. 1

This waltz has only one melody.

WALTZ NO. 2

The first melody of this waltz has already been given. The second melody follows:

WALTZ NO. 3 (FIRST MELODY)

The second melody of this waltz is omitted in this arrangement.

WALTZ NO. 4 (FIRST MELODY)

WALTZ NO. 4 (SECOND MELODY)

WALTZ NO. 5

The first melody of this waltz is omitted in this arrangement. The second melody follows:

1. Do you think that this waltz by Johann Strauss can be used for dancing, or is it more satisfactory for concert performance?
2. Have you noticed any things in the styles of writing of Johann Strauss and Richard Strauss which are alike?

Irish Washerwoman

[V. R. G 511 B

Irish Folk Dance, arranged by Leo Sowerby.

The music of this Irish dance is probably as well known in America as in Ireland. It is sometimes called an Irish jig, which means that it is a brisk dance in 6/8 measure and is very merry and jolly. Indeed probably no other dance music is more gay than the Irish jig.

The name "Washerwoman" indicates that it is a dance of occupation. On page 13, under "Folk Song," we learned that much of the folk music in any country centers around the interests, habits, and customs of the people. The definite rhythm of this dance and its happy carefree spirit describe a very lively washerwoman.

The jig took its name from an instrument something like a violin called the *Geige* (gī′gĕ). It is easy to imagine the dancers as they swing in and out, change partners, and altogether have a rollicking time.

THE MUSIC

Although nearly everyone has heard this tune, it is given here so that it will be easier to follow the musical arrangement.

The Irish Washerwoman

This melody consists of two separate phrases; and each phrase is heard six times, with many changes in instruments, tempo, and harmony. Here is a description of the changes in these phrases at their different appearances:

First Appearance. The first-phrase melody is played by the English horn with a staccato effect. The accompaniment by pizzicato strings, with responses from the wood winds, gives a vivid picture of the jerky steps of the jig. The second phrase is played by the violin, and the pizzicato accompaniment continues.

Second Appearance. Pizzicato strings and xylophone play the melody of the first phrase while the horns play a smooth accompaniment with sustained chords. The second phrase is played by the full orchestra, and the piccolo adds to the fun with little flourishes.

Third Appearance. The melody of the first phrase is heard in a lower register as the brass instruments play it with full chords. There is a retard at the end of the phrase, but the wood winds enter with the second phrase in the original tempo. New harmonies are heard as the music gradually comes to a complete stop at the end of the phrase.

Fourth Appearance. The music now has lost its jolly and lively feeling. It is more like a sentimental waltz and is played by the strings. An arpeggio* played by the piano leads to the second phrase, in which the clarinet plays the melody.

Fifth Appearance. The bassoon plays the melody of the first phrase, and wood winds are heard in the second phrase. Here, as in other appearances of the Irish folk dance, there are variations and decorations which make the arrangement very interesting. The accompaniment in this passage suggests the bagpipes.* Although the harp is generally thought of as the instrument of Ireland, the bagpipe is almost as popular there as in Scotland when used as an accompaniment for dancing.

Sixth Appearance. The brass instruments boldly play the first phrase and the full orchestra takes control of the second. The speed increases, and this arrangement of a familiar Irish folk dance ends with full, positive chords.

Robert McBride made an arrangement of an old tune in his "Fugato on a Well-Known Theme" (page 85).

1. Do you remember that sufficiently well to point out some ways in which Leo Sowerby's arrangement is like it?

2. Although "Irish Washerwoman," when played for a dance, must keep strictly to time, do you think it would be possible to make up any kind of dance for this arrangement?

THE ARRANGER

A single hearing of this music shows that the arranger is a modern thinker and treats his themes in a modern way. Leo Sowerby, although of British parentage, was born in Michigan. His music education began when he was still a little lad; in addition to his interest in the piano, he obtained a textbook and learned the rudiments of music.

Although most of his musical education has been received in the United States, he studied in Europe for three years and is one of the American musicians who won the Prix de Rome.

He enlisted in the American Army in the World War, and not only became a bandmaster but was promoted to second lieutenant.

He is expert in using modern devices. He has a certain liking for folk tunes and enjoys dressing them up in colorful harmonizations.

He tells an interesting story of how this composition came to be written:

> Many years ago, when I was quite a young man, I lived with a family in Chicago in whose household there was an Irish maid. She constantly heard me practicing on the piano the music of Beethoven, Bach, and the other masters, but apparently did not enjoy this sort of music. One day she said to me, "Why don't you ever play something that is really music?" I asked her what she had to suggest, and she replied, "Oh, some good old tune like the 'Irish Washerwoman.'"
>
> I told her that if she would buy a copy of it for me I would play it to her to her heart's content. This she did, and after I had become interested in the tune I made a transcription of it for piano which is the basis of the orchestral arrangement which Mr. Ormandy has recorded. I made the orchestral version of the piece shortly after I had written it for piano.

At the present time he is engaged in many musical activities. He is an organist of national reputation, a well-known composer, a teacher in the American Conservatory of Music in Chicago, and a lecturer. And he thoroughly enjoys it all.

Blue Danube Waltz

[V. R. 15425 A

JOHANN STRAUSS (1825–1899), Austrian composer.

This is one of the best known of all the waltzes by Johann Strauss. It is said that he composed anywhere and everywhere. As soon as a musical idea came into his head, down it went on a pad, the back of an envelope, or even on his cuff.

Can you name another composer who had a similar habit?

There are two stories about this music. One of them is that the principal melody of this set of waltzes came to the composer when he was preparing for a concert.

He wrote the theme on his cuff. By the end of the concert he had forgotten all about it. The shirt was sent to the laundry, but luckily his wife discovered before it was too late that a musical idea had been written on the cuff. She copied it, as was her custom, and then allowed the shirt to be washed.

The second story tells us that the *Blue Danube* became a kind of musical watchword in Vienna and was played on all social occasions. Brahms, the great composer, often used to attend the out-of-door concerts which Strauss conducted. On one occasion Mrs. Strauss asked the famous old composer to write his name on her fan. He wrote a few measures of the *Blue Danube* and added, "Unfortunately not by one Johannes Brahms."

THE MUSIC

This set of waltzes was first written as a number for a chorus, but it was not successful and was therefore arranged for orchestra. This seems strange, perhaps, as the chorus arrangement has been used so much in the schools in the United States. The opening words are "River so blue, so blue and bright."

As in the *Tales from the Vienna Woods*, the *Blue Danube* also is a series of five waltzes. A happy introduction ushers in the first waltz.

WALTZ NO. 1 (FIRST MELODY)

WALTZ NO. 1 (SECOND MELODY)

The second waltz is a complete little composition in itself, because the first melody returns after the second melody.

WALTZ NO. 2 (FIRST MELODY)

WALTZ NO. 2 (SECOND MELODY)

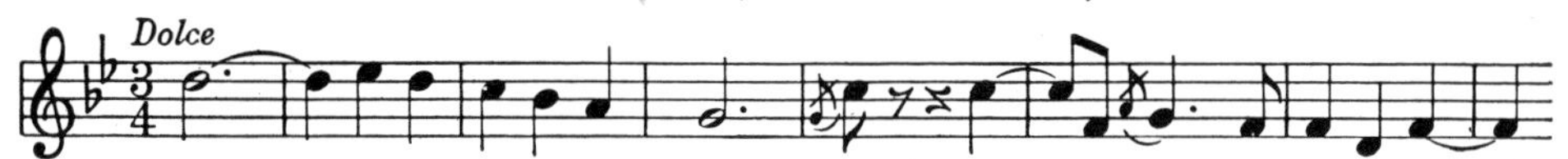

The third waltz enters without any introduction.

WALTZ NO. 3 (FIRST MELODY)

WALTZ NO. 3 (SECOND MELODY)

There is a short introduction to the fourth waltz.

WALTZ NO. 4 (FIRST MELODY)

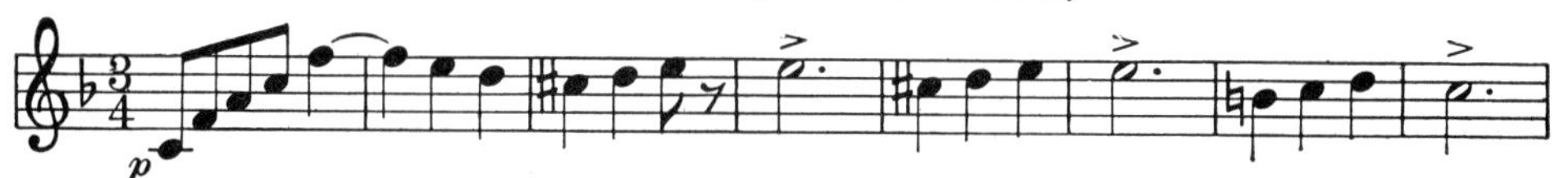

WALTZ NO. 4 (SECOND MELODY)[1]

The fifth waltz also has an introduction.

WALTZ NO. 5 (FIRST MELODY)

WALTZ NO. 5 (SECOND MELODY)

A coda brings this composition to a close.

JOHANN STRAUSS THE MAN

The first Johann Strauss, father of the composer of the *Blue Danube*, was a great favorite with the people of Vienna. He it was who first received the title of "Waltz King." He objected to letting any of his children go into the musical profession, but his son Johann was not to be turned aside. When only six years old he wrote his first waltz, and he had to keep his music lessons a secret because of his father's objections.

After a time Johann, Junior, organized a small orchestra and drilled it in his own compositions. When all was ready, he arranged to make his bow to the public in a large hall near Vienna. The city was filled with gossip, and the evening of the performance found the room crowded. The younger Strauss played, besides his own, some of his father's waltzes as a delicate honor to him, and the affair was a great success.

After his father died, the Johann Strauss who composed the music we have heard in this program of Rhythmic Melodies combined his own and his

[1] This melody is presented an octave lower than it appears in the score.

father's orchestras and went on a concert tour. He had other duties, but most of his attention was given to original composition. His music has made its way into all countries. In all he wrote about four hundred waltzes.

DISCUSSION

Many pieces of music belong in the class "When you first hear it you like it, and the more you hear it the better you like it." But it is not always possible to give the exact reason why we like a certain composition.

The word "waltz" suggests that each one of these Strauss compositions has naturally a strong rhythmic feeling.

1. Why does rhythmic music usually make a quicker appeal than some other kinds?
2. Do the melodies of the two Strauss waltzes seem alike in any way?
3. Do the melodies in each of the compositions hold interest?
4. Do any of these melodies seem especially attractive?

Johann Strauss has named in his titles some favorite spots of his own country: the Vienna Woods; the Danube River.

Does the music seem to have any close relation to the title? Or could you suggest some other titles which would be just as good?

Of course you have heard a great many waltzes, some for dancing and some for concert performance.

1. How do these waltzes by Johann Strauss compare with others that you know?
2. Can you give any reason as to why the *Blue Danube* is better known than *Tales from the Vienna Woods*?
3. Why do you think it continues to be so popular?
4. Have you any ideas as to why the waltz rhythm is such a favorite with composers?

It may be interesting to list the titles of all the waltzes which you know and like, and in a few words state why they are attractive to you.

14

MORE OPERA MUSIC

The story of *Hänsel and Gretel* has been given in connection with the program "Music and Fairy Tales" (page 55). At that time we listened to the overture to the opera and heard many of the songs played by the orchestra.

Three Songs from *Hänsel and Gretel* [V. R. 1948 A, B

Engelbert Humperdinck (1854–1921), German composer. *Living in America at the same time:* William Howard Taft.

Elisabeth Schumann, who sang the songs by Brahms and Schubert (page 94), has made a record of three songs from this delightful opera. They are:

Folk Song
Sandman's Lullaby
Evening Prayer

These songs all occur in the second act and follow each other in the order given.

The children are in the forest, and Hänsel is making a wreath of flowers while Gretel is looking for strawberries. She sings a simple folk tune that begins like this:

As Madame Schumann sings these songs in German (which, by the way, was the original language of the opera), the English translation is given here:

I. Folk Song. In the Forest

A tiny little man from the woodland stares;
A coat of purple cloth he wears.
Say, who could that fellow be,
Standing so still beneath the tree
With a purple jacket to his knee?

He stands on one leg, that queer chap,
And on his head is a little black cap.
Say, who could that fellow be,
Standing on one leg under the tree,
With a little cap as black as tea?

The solo starts immediately, without any introduction. The instrumental interlude between the two stanzas suggests bird songs in the forest.

After the song, Hänsel and Gretel keep on playing until night comes on. The darkness frightens them. In the beginning of the second scene some high soft notes prepare the way for the "Sandman's Lullaby." This is a very lovely tune, and the words explain how the sandman puts children to sleep.

II. Sandman's Lullaby

I am the Sandman, small and kind. Sh!
I have no wicked thought in mind. Sh!
I wrap the children in my spell, sh!
For I love little children well. Sh!
I enter at the nursery door,
Two tiny grains of sand I pour
Into each drowsy, drooping eye;
Then fast asleep the children lie.
And if they're good and hasten to obey,
On Heaven's dark heights
The stars will kindle lights;
And angel hosts will downward stream,
Bringing each child a happy dream.
Dream on, my children, dream away;
Dream holy dreams until the day.

THE MELODY

The melody moves along quietly and smoothly, and it seems as though the piano were singing too; for Ernest Lush, who plays the accompaniment, understands how much the piano part adds to this song. After a little we hear this phrase, which some people think is as lovely a bit of melody as Humperdinck ever wrote.

So the music gradually dies away. But before the children go to sleep they remember to say their prayers. The music and words for the "Evening Prayer" are given on pages 56–57.

This music is sung as a duet, and by one person, Elisabeth Schumann. This does not seem possible. But she first sang one part and it was recorded;

and then she sang the second part against her own voice. This is more than a stunt. To some people the fact that a person can sing a duet with herself is quite amazing; but the result is pleasing, and the singer has made a very attractive record.

1. Do these songs from *Hänsel and Gretel* have any qualities which we look for in an art song?
2. If you did not know the titles, would you be able to tell which of these songs is the folk song?
3. Do all these three melodies occur in the overture?

Overture to *The Marriage of Figaro* [V. R. 14325 A

WOLFGANG AMADEUS MOZART (1756–1791), Austrian composer. *Living in America at the same time:* ALEXANDER HAMILTON.

SCENES IN THE HOME OF A GENIUS

Shortly before our country was celebrating the tenth birthday of its Declaration of Independence, one of the very gifted and greatest men in the world of music was enjoying some of the most exciting experiences of his life in the city of Vienna.

Part of his excitement may have been due to the fact that he was very happy in his home life and that he and his wife were having a grand time. But Mozart was especially happy because of his opera *The Marriage of Figaro* (fĭg′ȧ-rō), upon which he was working with all possible speed and enthusiasm.

Mozart had played some of the music from *The Marriage of Figaro* to the Emperor (page 37), who liked it very much. This meant that the opera might be produced as soon as it could be finished. Now Mozart always composed very rapidly, and some of the stories of the speed with which he wrote music are almost unbelievable. But few of these stories are more surprising than the one told about this opera. It is said that Mozart composed the music for *The Marriage of Figaro* in only six weeks and, believe it or not, that he composed the overture only the evening before the first performance of the opera. Nowadays it would take an average composer several evenings merely to copy the manuscript, to say nothing of creating the music. However, Mozart was a genius; and a genius is always doing something which we cannot understand or explain.

But this was not all the excitement in the Mozart household. In fact the house was almost like a club, for singers were constantly dashing in to rehearse their parts for the new opera and to hear new music which Mozart would have ready for them. He was not only training them so that they could put on a good performance of his music, but he was actually composing it faster than they could learn it.

A SINGER TELLS OF A COMPOSER

All the people who describe those busy days in the Mozart home also tell that the singers were most enthusiastic over Mozart's music. This must have helped him very much in finishing his opera, for their pleasure in what he had written gave him new musical ideas.

One of the singers, an Irish tenor named Michael Kelly, has written an interesting account of these events, in which he says,

> All the original performers had the benefit of the instruction of the composer, who poured into their minds his inspired meaning. I shall never forget his little expressive face when lighted up with the shining rays of genius. It is as impossible to describe as it would be to paint a sunbeam.
>
> At the first rehearsal with the orchestra Mozart was on the stage with his crimson coat and gold-laced cocked hat, giving the time of the music to the orchestra.
>
> After one of the arias* the effect was like electricity itself, for all of the performers on the stage and those in the orchestra shouted, "Bravo, bravo, bravo Maestro! Viva, viva Grande Mozart!"

THE OVERTURE PREPARES FOR THE OPERA

We have already learned that composers often use the overture, or instrumental prelude, as a means of introducing some of the melodies which appear later in the opera. In fact, some composers have used these themes in the overture in such a way as to suggest the action with which they are associated in the opera. By arranging these themes in the overture in a certain order or by combining them in special ways composers can show the order of the important happenings in the opera itself.

Can you give the name of an opera in which the overture gives an idea of what goes on in the opera?

THE MUSIC

Although this overture does not contain any of the songs of the opera, it is a good idea to see and perhaps sing some of its important melodies.

The composition opens with measures of swirling notes which lead up to the first melody.

FIRST MELODY

There is a sudden change in the volume of the music as the entire orchestra seems to join in completing this tune.

The music moves merrily on until we hear the low instruments playing this figure:

This figure is repeated many times by different instruments, until at last we hear the strings playing the second melody:

SECOND MELODY

This melody is repeated, and then all the music which we heard in the beginning returns. The music is not only merry; it really sparkles with rapid runs and many sforzando* chords.

DISCUSSION

A good opera must have marked contrasts both in the action and the music.

1. After hearing the overture to *The Marriage of Figaro* do you have any idea of what takes place in the opera?

2. Do you find that there are changes in the tempo and in the character of the melodies?

3. If so, how would you describe them?

4. Are these changes so clear that they can suggest different people and scenes in the opera?

5. If so, how would you describe them?

6. If not, then would you say that this overture does not give any idea of what goes on in the opera?

A composer is not obliged to use tunes from his opera in the overture. Sometimes he merely wishes the overture to prepare the audience for the kind of opera which is to follow, without using any of its music. In other words, he desires to "set the mood." In such a case he composes music for the overture which expresses some of the same feelings and thoughts which are most prominent throughout the opera. This enables the listener to get into the spirit of the opera and prepares him for whatever may happen.

One person wrote about this overture, "This is the merriest of all operatic overtures, for it laughs and romps itself away in less than five minutes."

1. What do you think about this description?
2. For what kind of opera do you think this would be a desirable introduction?
3. Can you make any suggestions for a play that might follow such an introduction?

THE STORY OF THE OPERA

Although a knowledge of the story of *The Marriage of Figaro* is not necessary to an enjoyment of the music of the overture, a little of it may be interesting.

The story comes from a French comedy. The hero is a Spanish count whose wife is the beautiful countess Rosina, but this does not prevent him from noticing other beautiful maidens. The servant of the count is none other than Figaro, and he is to marry Susanna, the maid of Rosina.

There are all kinds of secrets, plots and suspicions. Men disguise themselves as women, and women as men. This all takes time, and the marriage of Figaro and Susanna which was to have taken place at the opening of the opera, is postponed again and again. But it is brought about, fortunately, before the opera ends.

Although more than a century and a half has passed since Mozart wrote this music, *The Marriage of Figaro* still holds a very high place among the operas. Its grace, lightness, beauty, and merry fun prove that cheerfulness is an outstanding quality in Mozart's music and that his love for laughter found its way into much of his writing.

15

MUSIC OF LONG AGO

DURING our experiences in listening to music we have found that although many new instruments have been invented and made in the course of the years, the violin was one of the earliest ones and over a long period of time has been a favorite with many great composers as well as with a large number of performers, whether professional or amateur.

One of the greatest violinists of all time was Nicolò Paganini (pä-gä-nē′nē), who began to play in public when he was only nine years old. He composed music as well, and the composition we are going to hear illustrates his skill as a performer.

Moto Perpetuo

[V. R. 14325 B

NICOLÒ PAGANINI (1782–1840), Italian composer. *Living in America at the same time:* HENRY CLAY.

The English translation of the title of this music is "Perpetual Motion," which suggests that the music keeps on going and going with great speed as though it never would end.

Although Paganini wrote this piece to be played on the violin, it is performed here by the Minneapolis Symphony Orchestra, under the direction of Eugene Ormandy (ôr′män-dĭ), who also made the arrangement. As might be expected, he has given the swift-moving melody to the violins, while the other instruments play the accompaniment.

THE MUSIC

It is beyond the ability of any human being to sing this melody. The principal idea in this composition is rapid motion, and there is not a songlike passage in it. The accompaniment, too, seems to be nothing more than a background against which the speed of these notes stands out more clearly.

A single chord is played, and then the violins begin their merry chase in this fashion:

In spite of the fact that the music moves so quickly that we are almost out of breath trying to keep up with it, we can recognize the passage which begins with these measures each time that it returns. There are many changes in volume from soft to loud and back again, and in some places the accents are much stronger than in others.

THE COMPOSER

Paganini was known as a *virtuoso.* That means that he excelled in skill as a performer. He was an amazing person and fairly dazzled his audiences with his remarkable ability. In other ways too he was rather odd, and he greatly enjoyed the widespread attention he received all over Europe. He was so far in advance of other violinists of his time that he was obliged to compose his own music to show off his ability. No one else could write music that was difficult enough to please him. He was master of his instrument, and those who have come after him have received great benefit from his ideas and from practicing his music.

1. Do you think it requires greater skill for a group than for a solo player to play "Perpetual Motion"?
2. Would it be possible to give this composition a different name which would describe it just as well?

Air and Gavotte from Orchestral Suite No. 3, in D Major

[V. R. 12010 A, B

Johann Sebastian Bach (1685–1750), German composer. *Living in America at the same time:* **Benjamin Franklin.**

A FAMOUS MELODY

One of the most famous of all melodies is the "Air" which Bach composed as a part of this Suite No. 3. You may remember that one of the movements of the suite by Henry Purcell was called "Song Tune"; "Air" means the same thing. Long ago this word was used in place of "melody."

Some melodies are great but not popular, while others may be popular but not very great. The melody of this "Air," however, has the honor of being both great and popular.

It is popular because it is familiar to nearly everyone. Perhaps one reason for its popularity is the fact that there is a familiar arrangement of it in which the entire melody is played upon one string of the violin. Since this string, the G string, gives the lowest tones that are possible on a violin, the melody is often heard at a lower pitch and has a darker and deeper tone quality than the composer intended. Bach wrote it, not for a low pitch, but for a high instrument. On this record we hear the melody as the composer indicated it should be played.

The melody is tender, yet it has strength, the kind of strength we associate with worthy character. It is dignified, yet it possesses those characteristics that make it easily understood. It is human, yet it has a nobility which is more than human.

This is music that can satisfy our deepest desires for those things which are far beyond us and are greater than we. For it draws from us the finest feelings and thoughts we can have, and through it we know that life can be rich and noble and beautiful.

THE MUSIC

Here are the opening measures of this famous melody:

The accompaniment to this melody is quite important. The bass moves over skips of an octave in this fashion:

But even though on the printed page it seems to skip about, it really moves in a smooth, steady, and dignified manner.

THE COMPOSER

No word of praise is needed for the man who composed this music. His music is great because he was great. But he was a modest, humble God-fearing man, though a great composer; and some of his most wonderful compositions came as an expression of his simple religious faith.

Sometimes Bach thrills us with his remarkable skill in writing fugues. At other times he overpowers us with his impressive and magnificent sacred choruses. But Bach speaks to us most beautifully in many of his smaller compositions, such as this Air from his Suite No. 3. This is one of the most friendly of all of Bach's compositions. In it we find a melodic loveliness which makes us ever grateful to the man who created it.

This man, the great Bach, lived quietly and wrote his music without thought of fame. Much of it was written to be performed in the church where he was organist (page 93); some of it was composed at the request of the nobility.

While Bach wrote most of his music over two hundred years ago, much of it has been known to concert audiences for only half that time. In fact this suite was not performed (except by the composer) until it was discovered and conducted by Mendelssohn (page 64), more than a hundred years after it was composed.

Between the time when this suite was written and the date of its first performance after Bach's death, the thirteen American colonies had become permanently established, freed themselves from England, founded the United States of America, and expanded into western territory.

Bach is often called the father of modern music. This may be a bit unfair to the composers who came before him, but it is true that there is practically nothing in the music of the present time, no matter how modern and up-to-date it may be, that cannot be traced in one way or another back to the music of Bach.

It is certain that after the work of Bach, music never again was the same. He improved the system of tuning for keyboard instruments (clavichord, harpsichord, and organ), and he introduced the first use of the thumb in playing on them. He wrote modern music for his time, and he made concert music out of the dance tunes of his day, two centuries before George Gershwin and Paul Whiteman ever thought of it.

GAVOTTE

One of these dance tunes was the *gavotte* (gȧ-vŏt′). This dance is the third movement of the Suite in D Major.

The gavotte is a French dance. It first became known in the sixteenth century and was very popular among the peasants. Later on, it gained the favor of royalty and became one of the most popular of court dances. It is said to have been a great favorite of Marie Antoinette (mȧ-rē′ äɴ-twȧ-nĕt′). As a peasant dance, the gavotte was lively and full of energy; but when it was danced at court, it became slower and more sober.

In this suite there really are two gavottes, although the composer did not give them separate titles. After each of the gavottes has been played, the first one is repeated.

What is the name that is often given to music written in this way?

The gavotte is always in duple* meter. It begins on the last half of a measure and ends with the first half of a measure. Each gavotte in the third movement of this suite is divided into two sections, and each of these sections is repeated.

At the beginning of the first gavotte we hear this melody:

FIRST MELODY

We can see Bach's skill in handling a melody, for the second section of the first gavotte opens with a clever inversion of the first melody.

SECOND MELODY

The inversion of a melody is like an inversion in fractions, for $\frac{1}{2}$ inverted becomes $\frac{2}{1}$. "Inversion" simply means turning something upside down; for example, standing on your head. Suppose you try holding a pencil in your hand with the eraser on top. Then turn the pencil over so that the eraser is at the bottom and the point is up. It is still the same pencil, isn't it? This is true also of melodies, and in this gavotte the second melody really is the first one turned upside down. High notes have become low ones, and low ones high. Rising phrases have become falling ones, and falling phrases rising ones.

As you look at the two melodies, can you see how Bach has done this?

We know that the second gavotte has arrived when we hear this melody:

THIRD MELODY

There is a second section in this gavotte, the melody being made up of parts of the third melody. The low instruments begin it.

FOURTH MELODY

1. How does the rhythm of the gavotte differ from that of the minuet; for example, the minuet from Haydn's Symphony No. 13?

2. Which of the two dances seems to be the livelier?

3. We have heard only two movements from this suite by Bach, and the entire suite by Purcell. Is there any difference between them?

4. How would you describe the important differences between the music of Bach's Suite No. 3, in D Major, and Tchaikovsky's *Nutcracker Suite*?

16

THE CONDUCTOR'S SCORE

ON THE two pages following is a reproduction of pages 68 and 69 in the *Nutcracker Suite*, by Tchaikovsky. It is of the same type as that which is used by the conductor of a symphony orchestra. This score includes all the notes which are played by all the instruments in the measures which are quoted. The individual players, however, use music which includes only the notes for their particular instruments.

These pages of score are from the Russian dance entitled "Trépak." They occur near the end of the dance, beginning twenty-eight measures before the "Trépak" is concluded. Each page of score which is reproduced contains six measures of music.

The two staves at the top of the pages, which are connected by a bracket, are for the flutes, of which there are three. It may be seen that all three flutes play the same note in some places.

Below the flutes is the part for the oboe (ō′bō). Below this is the staff marked "C. Ingl." This is the abbreviation for *Corno Inglese* (kôr′nō ēn-glā′sā), which means "English horn."

The next two staves, which are connected with a bracket, are for the two clarinets, below which the staff for the bass clarinet may be seen.

"Fg." is the abbreviation for *Fagotti* (få-gŏt′tē), which means "bassoons," of which there are two in this selection.

Since the French horns are sometimes grouped with the wood winds and at other times grouped with the brasses, their notes lie between the wood-wind and brass sections. This score calls for four French horns, and their parts are written on two staves, which are connected with a bracket and marked "Cor.," which is the abbreviation for *Corni* (kôr′nē), meaning "horns."

Below the horns we find the staff for the trumpets, "Trbe." being the abbreviation for *Trombe* (trŏm′bā), which means "trumpets."

How many trumpets are called for in this score?

The next two staves, which are connected with a bracket, are for the trombones and tuba. The score calls for three trombones. The notes for the first two are on the upper staff, while the third trombone plays the upper notes on the lower staff. The lower notes on the lower staff are played by the tuba.

These pages call for two staves for the percussion section. The abbreviation "Timp." is for *Timpani* (tĭm′på-nē). This score shows that two

68
60
Fl.
Ob.
C.Ingl.
Cl.
Cl.b.
Fg.
a 2
Cor.
Trbe.
Tbni.
Tuba
Timp.
Tamb.
Vl.
Vle.
Celli
C.-B.

Fl.
Ob.
C.Ingl.
Cl.
Cl. b.
Fg.
Cor.
Trbe.
Tbni.
Tuba
Timp.
Tamb.
Vl.
Vle.
Celli
C.-B.

timpani are used simultaneously and that different pitches are designated for them, for the timpani may be tuned to various pitches. The part for the tambourine, however, is written entirely on one space in the staff, since this instrument is not tuned.

Below the staff for the tambourine we find the music for the string section. The two upper staves, which are connected with a bracket, are for the first and second violins. The first violins play the upper staff and the second violins play the lower staff, and it may be seen that in some measures they are playing the same music an octave apart.

At what point in the score does this relationship cease?

"Vle.," which marks the third staff from the bottom of the page, is an abbreviation for *Viole* (vē-ō′lā), meaning "violas," which play a part similar to the other stringed instruments.

The cellos play the upper of the two staves which are joined with a bracket at the bottom of the pages. The lowest line of the score is for contrabasses, or bass viols, which sound an octave lower than the printed notes.

THE MUSIC

The principal melody which is given on these pages is the one which is quoted on page 44. It is played by the three flutes, the two clarinets, the first and second violins, and the violas. In the first three measures the other instruments merely provide harmonic and rhythmic effects. In the last three measures of page 68 of the score, however, the instruments which previously had the melody are joined by the oboes and cellos; and these instruments strengthen the most important notes of the melody, though they do not duplicate everything the other instruments play. The music on page 69 is a continuation and partial repetition of that on page 68.

THE CLEFS

In order that the lines and spaces of the staff may be connected with definite tones, it is necessary to have some sort of key which will fix the pitch of these lines and spaces. Therefore *clef* signs are used. *Clef* means "key," and the clef sign at the beginning of the staff fixes the pitch of a note on a certain line. For example, the treble, or G, clef fixes the pitch of G on the second line. Similarly, in the bass clef the pitch of F is fixed on the fourth line.

These pages of score use four clefs. The sign at the beginning of the line for the first and second trombones is called the tenor clef. The upper and lower sections of this clef meet on the fourth line and this means that middle C is located on the fourth line.

The sign at the beginning of the line for violas is called the alto clef, though it is more commonly known as the viola clef. The upper and lower sections of this clef meet on the third line, so middle C is located on the third line.

Both the tenor clef and the alto clef are used in order to avoid writing the added, or "leger," lines which would be necessary if only the treble and bass clefs were used. Added lines may be seen in the cello part on this page, and these lines could be avoided if the tenor clef were used, so as to bring middle C down on to the staff.

KEY SIGNATURES

Perhaps you have noticed that several of the lines for various instruments have different key signatures. This is due to the fact that certain instruments are made in such a way that if they were playing the same written note, they would sound different tones. For example, if the violin and the B-flat clarinet were both to play the same written note, the clarinet would sound a tone lower than the violin. Therefore, if the clarinet is to sound the same tone as the violin, its note must be written a tone higher than that for the violin. For this reason, the clarinet is known as a transposing instrument, since the violin plays the actual pitch of the written note, and the clarinet does not. The B-flat clarinet is so called because it produces a B flat when its written note is C, and other transposing instruments are named according to the same principle.

Reading the score from top to bottom, the first of these transposing instruments is the English horn. This instrument is made in such a way that it sounds a fifth lower than the written note it plays. For this reason its notes must be presented in a key a fifth higher than that at which they are intended to sound. On these pages of score the music is in the key of G; therefore the part for the English horn must be written in the key which is a fifth higher, namely, D.

The clarinets which are used in this particular selection are in A rather than B flat. Since the A clarinet sounds a minor third lower than the written note, this part is written in the key of B flat, which is a minor third higher than G, the key of the selection.

For a similar reason, the part of the bass clarinet is a ninth higher than it sounds. The notes for the French horn are written with the same change of key as the English horn, and in this selection the trumpets are written with the same change of key as the clarinets.

In these pages of score, however, no key signature is used for the horns and trumpets, the sharps and flats being written in where necessary.

Diagram of Composers Represented in This Book

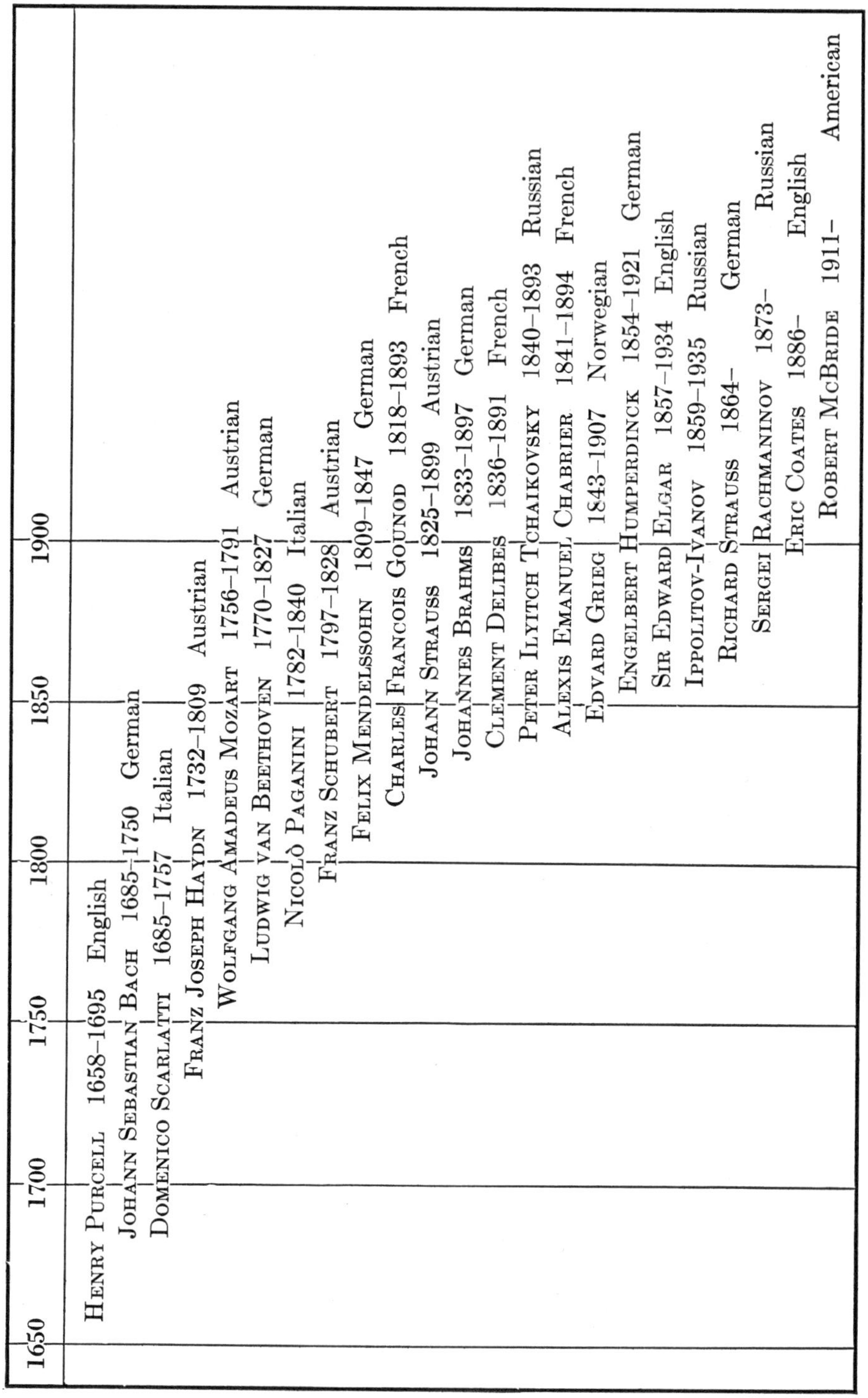

1650 · 1700 · 1750 · 1800 · 1850 · 1900

Composer	Dates	Nationality
Henry Purcell	1658–1695	English
Johann Sebastian Bach	1685–1750	German
Domenico Scarlatti	1685–1757	Italian
Franz Joseph Haydn	1732–1809	Austrian
Wolfgang Amadeus Mozart	1756–1791	Austrian
Ludwig van Beethoven	1770–1827	German
Nicolò Paganini	1782–1840	Italian
Franz Schubert	1797–1828	Austrian
Felix Mendelssohn	1809–1847	German
Charles Francois Gounod	1818–1893	French
Johann Strauss	1825–1899	Austrian
Johannes Brahms	1833–1897	German
Clement Delibes	1836–1891	French
Peter Ilyitch Tchaikovsky	1840–1893	Russian
Alexis Emanuel Chabrier	1841–1894	French
Edvard Grieg	1843–1907	Norwegian
Engelbert Humperdinck	1854–1921	German
Sir Edward Elgar	1857–1934	English
Ippolitov-Ivanov	1859–1935	Russian
Richard Strauss	1864–	German
Sergei Rachmaninov	1873–	Russian
Eric Coates	1886–	English
Robert McBride	1911–	American

17

MUSICAL WORDS AND EXPRESSIONS EXPLAINED

Absolute music: Instrumental music which depends upon its own melodies, harmonies, rhythms, and form for its appeal, without any help from a story or program. Absolute music is sometimes called *pure music,* or *abstract music.*

Accompaniment: Music which supports and enriches a vocal or instrumental melody is called the accompaniment. It may merely supply a harmonic background for the melody, or it may be an equal partner of the solo part, supplying contrasting melodies and other interesting material. It may be furnished by one or more instruments, or by a chorus, or by a combination of voices and instruments.

Adagio (ȧ-dä'jō): The Italian word for "very slowly." It is a term of expression which may also be used as the title of a piece of music, or of a movement in a large instrumental composition. It usually suggests that the music is to be played not only slowly, but with much expression.

Allegretto (äl-lā-grĕt'tō): The diminutive of *allegro.* It means not quite as fast as *Allegro,* but faster than *Andante.*

Allegretto grazioso (äl-lā-grĕt'tō grä-tsē-ō'sō): Moderately fast and in a graceful manner.

Allegretto scherzando (äl-lā-grĕt'tō skĕr-tsän'dō): A term of expression meaning "moderately quick and playful."

Allegretto tempo di valse (äl'lā-grĕt'tō tĕm'pō dē vȧls): Moderately rapid waltz time.

Allegretto tranquillo e grazioso (äl-lā-grĕt'tō trän-kwē'lō ā grä'tsē-ō'sō): Moderately quick, quiet and graceful.

Allegro (äl-lā'grō): An Italian word which means "cheerful," "moderately quick," or "lively." This term of expression is used as the title of a brisk movement in a symphony or other instrumental work.

Andante (än-dän'tā): This Italian word means "going," "walking"; and so, as a term of expression, suggests "rather slowly and gracefully." It often appears also as the title of the slow movement in a symphony or sonata.

Andante ma non troppo (än-dän'tā mä nŏn trôp'pō): Slow and graceful, but not too slow.

Andantino (än-dän-tē'nō): The diminutive of *andante,* indicating a more rapid tempo.

Aria (ä'rĭ-ȧ): A melody, sometimes very elaborate, for a single voice with accompaniment.

Arpeggio (är-pĕd'jō): A broken chord; one in which the notes are played one after another.

Arrangement: A rewriting of a composition to make it simpler or more elaborate, or to make it suitable for performance by a medium of expression other than that for which it was originally written.

Art song: The opposite of a folk song. Usually one in which the music has been carefully composed to express the meaning and spirit of the poem. Very often the music is different for each stanza.

Assai (äs-sä'ē): "Very."

Bagpipe: A wind instrument consisting of a leather bag and four or more pipes, with a single or double reed. The bag is filled with wind blown from the mouth of the player or from a pair of bellows worked by the arm. It is a very ancient instrument and was invented in some Oriental country. It was known to the Greeks and the Romans, and is still popular in Scotland and Ireland.

Ballet (băl-ā'): An elaborate dance or set of dances performed by trained dancers in appropriate costumes before an audience. It may take place at some convenient point in an opera or may be given independently. It may tell a story, or it may give pleasure merely by the grace of the dancers' motions, by the beauty of their patterns of movement as a group, and by the way in which these are fitted to the music which (nearly always) accompanies the ballet.

Bass Drum: A large drum with parchment heads, each stretched over a hoop and held in place by a larger hoop. When struck, it produces a deep sound without definite pitch.

Bassoon: A large instrument of the woodwind choir. It consists of a conical wooden tube so long that it is doubled back on itself, and has a long, bent mouthpiece. The tone is produced by the vibration of a double reed. The bassoon is usually the bass of the woodwind. Its tone is somewhat like that of the violoncello, but with a rather reedy quality.

Bells: A set of hollow steel tubes, graduated in size and suspended from a wooden framework. They are accurately tuned, and the tone is produced by striking the upper end of the tubes with a hammer.

Cadence: From a Latin word meaning "to fall"; the part of a phrase which seems to settle down to a point of rest, or a close, either temporary or final. In ancient music and in most folk music, the last notes of a melody usually *fall* toward their close. In modern music this is much less often true, yet the word *cadence* is still used for the ending of a part or the whole of a melody.

Cadenza: A brilliant passage in a vocal or instrumental piece, which gives the performer a chance for the display of skill. In old operatic music, this opportunity was usually given just before the close of a song; hence the term *cadenza,* which is the Italian form of the word *cadence.* A cadenza often occurs in a concerto, usually unaccompanied, and frequently makes use of the chief themes of the movement.

Canon: From a Greek word which means "rule"; a composition in which the melody is first given in one part, or voice, and then repeated by other parts on a different pitch, exactly according to rule. The second part begins a few beats after the first, the third part a few beats after the second, and so on, so that there is an effect of overlapping voices. A canon is the strictest kind of musical imitation. The simplest form of a canon is a round.

Cantabile (kän-tä'bē-lā): A term of expression meaning that the music is to be performed in a graceful, singing style.

Castanets: Small ivory or wooden shells held in the hand and clicked together. They have no fixed musical pitch, and are used merely to mark the rhythm. They originated in Spain.

Celesta: A keyboard instrument with a compass of five octaves. Bars of steel are suspended over wooden boxes called resonators, and pressing a key causes a hammer to strike a bar. The action is much like that of a piano, and the tone is clear, delicate, and sweet.

Choir: One of the distinct sections of a symphony orchestra: the strings, brass, or woodwind; also, a group of organized singers, especially in a church.

Chord: Three or more tones of different pitches sounded together, producing harmony. The tones may or may not seem to blend with a pleasing sound.

Chromatic: A half step above or below the pitch belonging to the key indicated in the signature. A chromatic scale is made up wholly of half steps. *Chromatic* literally means "colored," and the use of flats and sharps (other than those belonging to the key of the music) affects the tone color of a composition.

Clarinet: A woodwind instrument in the form of a cylindrical tube with a flaring end, having a single reed. It is an instrument with a wide range, variety of tone color and volume, and is considered the most useful and in some ways the most beautiful of the woodwinds. In its lowest register the tone is hollow and dark; in the middle register the tone is weak; in the upper register, clear and tender.

Classic overture: An overture is an instrumental prelude to an opera or oratorio or other similar work. A classic overture is an independent composition, consisting of three sections which show contrast in rhythm and style.

Clavichord: A keyboard instrument which was a direct forerunner of the piano. It was widely used in the sixteenth, seventeenth, and eighteenth centuries. The tone, which was very soft and delicate, was produced by small pieces of metal, called *tangents,* striking upward against the strings when the player struck the keys of the instrument.

Clavier: A keyboard; also the name applied by the Germans to a piano or other instrument with a keyboard.

Climax: The place where the music reaches the greatest degree of impressiveness or force; the high point of a composition.

Coda: This comes from the Latin word for "tail." In early music it meant a few strong chords used at the close of a piece of music to make an effective ending. The coda may be an interesting section by itself, especially in a sonata or symphony, in which it may act as a climax and sum up the whole movement.

Codetta: As you would expect, this word means "a little coda." It differs from a coda only in length. The word is also used to designate a connecting passage in a fugue.

Comic opera: An opera with a humorous plot. Often, in comic opera, some of the words are spoken, in contrast to grand opera, in which there is no spoken dialogue.

Con anima (kōn ä'nē-mä): With energy.

Con fuoco (kōn fŭ-ô'kō): With spirit.

Con moto (kōn mō'tō): "With spirited movement."

Concerto (kōn-chĕr'tō): An elaborate work, usually in three movements, giving an opportunity for display of the performer's skill and written for a solo instrument (or group of instruments) accompanied by an orchestra.

Contrabass: Another name for double bass, the largest and deepest-toned member of the string choir.

Contrapuntal: Written in the style, and according to the rules, of *counterpoint* (see next column).

Countermelody: A melody to be performed with another melody.

Counterpoint: The fitting together of two or more melodies. The term comes from the Latin words meaning "point against point," *point* being the old word for *note.*

Crescendo (krĕ-shĕn'dō): A term of expression meaning "with increasing power or volume of tone."

Cymbals: A pair of flat metal plates, or disks. They produce a bright, reverberating sound of indefinite pitch when their edges are struck together with a sliding movement.

Diatonic: Using only the tones of a standard major or minor scale; in contrast to *chromatic.*

Division: A section of a movement or piece, expressing a complete musical thought.

Dolce (dōl'chā): A term of expression meaning "sweetly," "softly."

Dolce cantando (dōl'chā kän-tän'dō): "In a sweet, songlike style."

Dolcissimo (dōl-chĭs'ĭ-mō): "With the utmost sweetness."

Double Bass: The largest member of the string choir and the fundamental bass of the symphony orchestra. It has four (sometimes five) strings, which are tuned in fourths; and it is played with a short, sturdy bow. The part is written an octave above the actual sound, in order to avoid the constant use of leger lines below the staff.

Drone bass: A bass part, consisting of two tones a fifth apart, which is continued through a piece or section of a piece.

Drum: See Bass Drum *or* Snare Drum.

Duple rhythm: Time in which the number of beats in a measure is exactly divisible by 2.

English horn: A member of the woodwind choir; the tone is produced by the vibration of a double reed. The English horn is half as long again as the oboe, and is pitched five tones lower. Actually it is an alto oboe, with a more somber tone than the oboe.

Ensemble (än-sŏm'b'l): The whole of the parts taken together, as in a combination of voices or instruments. The term very frequently refers also to a small group of soloists gathered together to play what is known as chamber music.

Entr'acte (än-trăkt'): Literally, "between acts"; a term applied to a piece of music or a dance given between the acts of a play or opera.

Espressivo (ĕs-prĕs-sē'vō): A term indicating that the music is to be played or sung "with expression."

Fandango: A Spanish dance in quick triple time, generally accompanied by castanets. It may be danced as a solo, or by one or more couples.

Fanfare: A flourish of trumpets.

Fantasia: An instrumental composition free in style or form; sometimes a piece founded on themes from an opera or upon folk tunes.

Figure: A small group of tones having a rhythmic or melodic pattern distinctive enough to be recognized easily.

Flute: An instrument consisting of an open cylindrical tube without a reed. The player blows across a hole in the side instead of blowing into the end, and plays by using finger holes and keys. It is the soprano instrument of the woodwind choir and the most agile of the wind instruments. It is capable of sweet, liquid tones.

Folk dance: A dance of the "folk," or people, which grew out of their natural activities and fondness for rhythmic expression. Many folk dances are vigorous, and often they reveal some of the racial traits of the people.

Folk song: A song of the people. Generally it has no known composer, but grew out of the emotions and everyday life of the "folk," or people. Many folk songs were originally folk dances, the words being added later. These songs express the joys and sorrows of the people, and often possess great beauty.

Form: The plan used by a composer in arranging his musical ideas. The term may refer to the plan of a single piece, or to that of a class or type of composition.

Forte (fôr'tā): A term of expression meaning "loudly." Abb. *f.*

Fortissimo (fôr-tĭs'ĭ-mō): A term of expression meaning "very loudly." Abb. *ff.*

French horn: An instrument consisting of a coiled brass tube about twelve feet long, ending with a large "bell," or flared mouth and having valves. The tone is produced by the vibration of the player's lips against the funnel-shaped mouthpiece. It is the most difficult to play of all the wind instruments. The tone is mellow and pleasing.

Fugato (fōō-gä'tō): "Like a fugue"; a composition following the general style of a fugue, but not observing strictly all its rules.

Fugue (fūg): From the Latin *fuga,* meaning "flight"; a composition in which there is a flight or chase of melodies, one part entering with the principal theme and followed by other parts repeating the same theme at certain distances according to fixed rules. The main divisions are called subject, answer, countersubject, and free parts.

Gamba (gäm'bä), or *Viola da gamba:* The bass instrument in the old family of viols, which preceded the modern violin and other stringed instruments. The gamba had six or seven strings. Its tone was not so pleasing as that of the violoncello, the instrument which has taken its place. However, the gamba continued to be popular longer than the other viols. All these instruments have been revived in recent times.

Giusto (jōō'stō): "Exact, strict."

Grace note: Tones are sometimes added to a vocal or instrumental melody to decorate it, and such added tones are given the general name *embellishments.* Grace notes are one form of embellishment; and are usually written in small notes, since they are played so quickly, and so that they may be easily recognized.

Grandioso (grän-dĭ-ō'sō): "Grand, noble."

Grazioso (grä-tsĭ-ō'sō): "Graceful, elegant."

Guitar (gĭ-tär'): A six-stringed instrument played by plucking the strings with the fingers. The body is shaped somewhat like that of a violin, and the finger board has frets, or raised lines, to show where the fingers should press to produce different tones. It is a very old instrument and is still widely used, especially in Spain.

Harmony: In general, any group or combination of tones; technically, the art of writing and using chords.

Harp: An instrument with strings set in an open frame. The player plucks the strings with a sweeping motion of the hands. The harp is tuned to the scale of C flat major, and a series of pedals alters the length of the strings as a means of changing the key. The harp was invented in very ancient times. It is not a regular member of the orchestra; but it can be used very effectively, and many modern composers write a part for it.

Harpsichord: A keyboard instrument with a harp-shaped frame. Pressing a key causes a quill to pluck a string. Like the clavichord, it was an ancestor of the piano.

Imitation: The repetition, exact or slightly changed, of a theme or figure already stated in a different part, or voice. This device is very strikingly used in the canon and the fugue.

Incidental music: Music to be performed in connection with a play or other dramatic work, to enhance its effect.

Instrumentation: Instruments selected to play together, as in an orchestra or a band. The term is also used to mean the art of writing or arranging music to be played by a band or orchestra.

Interlude: A short instrumental passage played between parts of a church service, between the acts of a drama, between the sections of a song or aria, or between the sections of an instrumental selection.

Intermezzo (ĭn-tẽr-mĕd′zō): Italian for "interlude"; a light composition played between the acts of an opera or drama, to allow the hearers to relax or to prepare the mood of the next act; an *entr'acte.* The title is also used for an independent composition.

Interval: The difference in pitch between two tones.

Introduction: A preliminary section which prepares the mind of the listener for the composition to follow. An introduction may be simple or elaborate, short or long.

Invention: The name given by Bach to fifteen small contrapuntal clavichord or harpsichord pieces in two voices, or parts.

Jota (hō′tä): A Spanish dance in quick triple rhythm. It is somewhat like a waltz, but the steps are more varied.

Kettledrums (*Timpani*): A pair of metal bowls over which parchment heads are stretched. The tension of the head is changed by means of screws or pedals, producing a change of pitch. Generally they are tuned to the first or fifth of the scale. They can produce tones varying in volume from a mere tap to a thunderclap.

Key: A system of scale tones built on a selected tone. The key takes its name from the first tone of the scale. There are a major and a minor form of each key.

Larghetto (lär-gĕt′tō): "Rather slowly."

Largo (lär′gō): "Slowly and broadly."

Legato (lā-gä′tō): "Smooth," "even," "flowing." It is the opposite of *staccato.*

Leggiero (lĕd-jā′rō): "Light," "nimble," "swift."

Lento (lĕn′tō): "Slowly."

Libretto (lĭ-brĕt′ō): The text or words of an opera, oratorio, or cantata.

Lute: A stringed instrument which was invented very long ago. It had a pear-shaped body and a long neck, and the number of strings was changed from time to time during the many years that the lute was in popular use. Its tones, which were mellow and full, were produced by plucking the strings.

Major: The Latin word meaning "greater." When applied to a scale, it indicates one in which the third tone is two whole steps above the keynote. Such a scale is said to be in the *major mode.*

Marcatissimo (mär-kä-tĭs'ĭ-mō): "Very strongly accented."

Marcato (mär-kä'tō): "With emphasis."

March: A piece of music, often in four-quarter measure, with a strongly marked rhythm which makes it suitable for marching.

Marziale (mär-tsĭ-ä'lā): "Martially," or "in the style of a march."

Measure: The unit of time or metrical division between two bars. All measures following a time signature are of equal length, and each measure has strong and weak accents in a given pattern.

Melodic subject: The principal theme of a section or of a composition.

Melody: A pleasing series of single tones having some sort of key relationship and a rhythmic design.

Meter: A term used both of music and of poetry. In music it has reference to the regular grouping of tones, or to the rhythmic plan of a particular work.

Metronome: A mechanism for marking tempo. It usually consists of an inverted pendulum with a sliding weight. This pendulum sways to and fro a certain number of times a minute. When the weight is moved up, thus lengthening the pendulum, the rate of motion is slower; when moved down, shortening the pendulum, the rate is faster.

Mezzo forte (mĕd'zō fôr'tā): "Half loud"; "moderately loudly." Abbr. *mf.*

Mezzo piano (mĕd'zō pē-ä'nō) "Half soft"; "moderately softly." Abbr. *mp.*

Minor: Literally, "less" or "smaller." When applied to a scale, it indicates one in which the third tone is one and one-half steps above the keynote. Such a scale is said to be in the *minor mode.*

Minuet: A graceful and stately French dance in three-quarter measure. The minuet has been much used as a number in the suite, and also as a movement in the sonata and symphony.

Mode: Style or kind of scale; the manner of arranging whole and half steps to form a scale. The best-known modes are the major and the minor.

Moderato (mŏd'ĕ-rä'tō): "At a moderate speed."

Moderato assai (mŏd'ĕ-rä'tō ä-sä'ē): Very moderately.

Modulation: The gradual change from one key, or *tonality,* to another by using a succession of chords.

Molto (mōl'tō): "Much," "very."

Molto vivace (mōl'tō vē-vä'chā): Very quick and lively.

Mood: A state of feeling.

Motive: A melodic or rhythmic theme on which a composition or a movement may be constructed. The term is also used to describe a division of a phrase.

Movement: A division, usually complete in itself, of a large work such as a sonata or symphony.

Music drama: The name applied by Richard Wagner to his later operas. These were intended to be examples of a new art form, in which drama, stage settings, orchestra, and voices were all blended into an artistic whole.

Musical motto: A phrase in a musical composition which has the same meaning as a motto does in a story or essay.

Mute: A device to deaden or to change the sound of an instrument. A clamp of brass, ivory, or wood is used for this purpose with the violin, viola, violoncello, or double bass. A leather-covered pad is one of the mutes used with brass instruments.

Nobilmente (nō-bĭl-mĕn'tā): Nobly, or in a grand manner.

Nocturne: Literally, "night piece"; an instrumental composition of romantic and reflective nature, for one or more instruments.

Note: A written or printed symbol representing a tone.

Oboe: An instrument consisting of a conical tube with a flaring end. The tone is produced by the vibration of a double reed, and the pitch is controlled by the use of finger holes and keys. The low and high registers are seldom used, but in the middle register the tone, though penetrating, is flexible and pleasing.

Octave: A series of eight consecutive diatonic tones (that is, tones of the major or minor scale) or the interval between any tone and the same tone eight staff degrees above or below it.

Opera: A drama set to music for soloists and chorus, with appropriate costumes, scenery, and action, and accompanied by an orchestra.

Oratorio: A drama, usually on a religious subject, set to music for chorus and soloists, and accompanied by an orchestra. It is performed without scenery or action.

Orchestra: A group of trained musicians playing together, with a leader called a *conductor*. A full orchestra consists of four sections: strings, woodwinds, brasses, and percussion instruments. In the symphony orchestra the first three sections are sometimes called *choirs*. The string choir consists of first and second violins, violas, violoncellos, and double basses. In a typical symphony orchestra two thirds of the players belong to the string choir. The woodwind choir includes piccolos, flutes, oboes, English horns, clarinets, and bassoons. The brass choir consists of trumpets, French horns, trombones, and tubas. Percussion instruments include drums, timpani, cymbals, triangles, bells, castanets, and other instruments which produce rhythmic effects. This section is often called the *battery*. The orchestra may include other instruments, such as the harp, organ, piano, celesta, and so on. The combination of instruments varies with different orchestras and with different compositions.

Organ: A wind instrument consisting of many pipes of different kinds and sizes, with tones and volume of great variety. It has one or two or more keyboards (called *manuals*) and pedals (which, in the organ, are really an extra keyboard played upon by the feet). The pipes are caused to sound by compressed air provided by bellows or electrical blowers, and are controlled by "stops." The organ is the largest of instruments and exceeds all others in grandeur and variety of tone.

Organ point: See *Pedal point.*

Overture: An orchestral introduction to a play, an opera, or an oratorio; or, sometimes, the opening portion of a symphony or other instrumental work. The title is also given to an independent composition.

Pedal point: A tone which is continued, usually in the bass, while the other parts move freely. The sustained tone is often the keynote, often the fifth tone of the scale. This is also known as *organ point.*

Percussion: From the Latin word meaning "to strike"; applied to instruments in which the sound is produced by a blow, or stroke, such as drums, timpani, bells, and so on.

Period: A division of a movement or piece which comes to a definite close. It is a complete musical sentence.

Phrase: A division of a piece of music, often four or eight measures in length. Two or more phrases make a period.

Pianissimo (pĕ-ȧ-nĭs'ĭ-mō): A direction meaning "very softly." Abbr. *pp.*

Piano (pĕ-ä'nō): "Softly." Abbr. *p.*

Pianoforte, or *Piano*: A stringed instrument and also an instrument of percussion, with a range slightly over seven octaves. The tone is produced by the vibration of steel wires struck by felt hammers operated from the keyboard. A sounding board gives added resonance. The tone can be varied in duration and intensity by the use of pedals, and the touch of the player is largely responsible for the beauty of the tone.

Piccolo: From the Italian *flauto piccolo,* meaning "little flute." It is about half the size of the flute and has a smaller range and a higher pitch. It is played in the same way, and is characterized by a shrill tone.

Pitch: The position of a tone in a musical scale; the height or depth of a musical tone.

Più moderato (pyōō mŏd-ĕ-rä'tō): "More moderately."

Più mosso (pyōō môs'sō): "More rapidly."

Pizzicato (pēt-sĭ-kä'tō): The Italian word for "pinched." In music it means that the player of a violin or other stringed instrument must pluck the strings with the fingers instead of using the bow.

Poco (pō'kō): "A little."

Postlude: A selection played on the organ at the end of a church service; also a few measures of the accompaniment at the close of a song, to make an effective and artistic ending.

Prelude: An instrumental introduction to an opera, oratorio, song, or other vocal work; the first movement of an instrumental suite; the introduction to a fugue; or the music played on the organ at the beginning of a church service. By some composers, such as Chopin and Rachmaninov, the name has been given to a short independent piece for piano.

Presto (prĕs'tō): "Quickly, rapidly."

Program music: Music which is based on a program suggesting a story or scene. The title serves as a guide to the listener's imagination in following the music.

Quartet: A sonata composed for four instruments, usually two violins, viola, and cello (a string quartet). Also, a group of musicians formed to play such music or to sing.

Range: The extent of the tones or pitches which a voice can sing or an instrument can play is called its range, or compass.

Recitative (rĕs-ĭ-tȧ-tēv'): A kind of musical recitation or declamatory singing; also a piece of music intended to be sung in this way. Sometimes, a piece of instrumental music resembling a vocal recitative in style.

Reed: The tone-producing part of a woodwind instrument and of some other instruments, such as the reed organ and the accordion. It consists of a thin, elastic strip of cane or metal, fastened at one end, and vibrates when a stream of air passes over it or, in the case of a double reed (*see* Bassoon, English horn, Oboe), between its halves.

Register: A distinct section of the range of a voice or of an instrument.

Related keys: Keys with a number of tones in common and having signatures that differ but slightly.

Repetition: A repeat, or reiteration.

Rhapsody: From the Greek, meaning "songs put together." Originally the rhapsody was a group of ballads combined to make an epic poem. It now means an instrumental piece without set form, often based on national airs or folk melodies.

Rhythm: The flow of regular pulsations in music; measured motion; regularity of movement marked by a succession of light and heavy accents.

Rondo: Originally a dance song with a refrain; now an instrumental piece with one principal theme which appears again and again, alternating with other themes.

Round: A kind of vocal canon, with the parts in unison or an octave apart.

Saxophone: A wind instrument consisting of a tapering tube flaring at the end. It has a single reed and a mouthpiece like that of the clarinet. There is a whole family of saxophones, of varying sizes.

Scale: From the Latin *scala,* meaning "stairway" or "ladder"; a series of tones a step or a half step apart within an octave, beginning with a tone of any given pitch and arranged according to a given pattern.

Scherzando (skĕr-tsän'dō): Playfully, jokingly.

Scherzo (skĕr'tsō): The Italian word for "joke." A light, vivacious piece of music; or a bright and rapid movement, usually in triple rhythm, in a symphony.

Score: A written or printed copy of a composition, with the parts arranged one above another and the staves connected by bars. In a piano score there are two staves so arranged. An orchestra score may require twenty or more staves.

Semistaccato: "In a rather detached, or disconnected, way."

Semplice (sĕm'plē-chā): "Simply, plainly."

Serenade: Originally applied to a song, but now used as a title for instrumental compositions of dreamy, romantic character.

Sforzando (sfôr-tsän'dō): "With special emphasis." Abbr. *sf.*

Signature: The signs and figures at the beginning of a composition. The clef sign and the sharps or flats make up the key signature; and the figures following, indicating the number of beats in a measure and the kind of note which is the unit of beat, are called the time or meter signature.

Snare drum: A smaller drum than the bass drum, with strings of rawhide (called snares) stretched across the lower head. The snares vibrate when the drum is beaten, giving a sound without definite pitch.

Sonata: An elaborate composition for a piano, violin, or other instrument, or for any two of such instruments, having three or four movements in related keys.

Song form: A musical composition made up of two contrasting themes, with the arrangement indicated by A B or A B A.

Staccato: Detached or disconnected; played in a way which leaves short intervals of silence between tones. It is the opposite of *legato.*

Staff (plural, *Staves*): The five parallel lines on or between which notes are placed to indicate their pitch.

Strophic: A term applied to a song which has the same melody and accompaniment for each of its stanzas.

Subject: A melody or musical theme which serves as the foundation of a composition or of a movement in a large work.

Suite: Originally a set of contrasting dances, from three to five in number, written in the same or related keys. A modern suite is an instrumental composition having as many divisions as the composer wishes. It is no longer restricted to dances, and is often based on a "program."

Symphony: A sonata composed for full orchestra.

Symphony orchestra: A full orchestra which has for its purpose the playing of symphonies and other large compositions. The instrumentation differs with the music which is performed.

Syncopation: A shifting of accent giving a strong accent to a beat which would naturally be unaccented.

Tambourine: A small flat drum with one parchment head and one uncovered side. The covered side may be struck with the hand, and bits of metal attached to the rim may be shaken against one another to make a jingling sound (or the thumb may be rubbed over the parchment to produce a similar effect).

Tarantella: A dance of southern Italy in 6/8 measure, performed with gradually increasing speed.

Tempo: The Italian word for "time"; the rate of speed with which a selection (or a section of it) is to be performed.

Tempo di marcia vivo (tĕm'pō dē mär'chä-vē'vō): "In the time of a lively march."

Theme: A melodic or rhythmic idea or subject.

Three-part form with trio: This is one kind of song form. The traditional plan is as follows: Part I is made up of two well-defined themes, each played twice. Part II also has two themes, different from those of the first part. It is known as the *trio,* because in the eighteenth century it was played by three instruments. Part III is a repetition of Part I, with the themes played only once.

Time signature: The figures on the staff at the beginning of a composition. The upper figure indicates the number of beats in the measure, and the lower figure indicates the kind of note which is the unit of beat. The word *time* is sometimes used instead of *meter,* and refers to the regular groupings of tones.

Timpani: *See* Kettledrums.

Tonality: Mode, key, or scale system.

Tone color: The quality which enables us to distinguish the tone of any instrument; also applied to the effect produced by different combinations of instruments or by the introduction of chromatics.

Tonic: The first note, or keynote, of a scale.

Tonic chord: The chord built on the tonic, or keynote.

Tranquillo (trän-kwēl'lō): "Calmly, quietly."

Transcription: An arrangement or adaptation of a composition, usually to enable it to be played on some other instrument than that for which it was written.

Transition: The change from one key or mode to another without preparation; also the name of a passage leading from one theme to another.

Transpose: To change the key of a composition, either when writing or performing, to one lower or higher in pitch.

Triangle: A small steel bar bent into triangular shape. When struck with a pencil-like rod it gives a high, bright sound.

Trio: A group of three performers, or the music, usually in sonata form, for such a group. Also, the middle or contrasting section of a march, minuet, waltz, or scherzo. *See* Three-part form with trio.

Triple rhythm: Meter in which the number of beats in a measure is 3 or 9, regardless of the kind of note receiving one beat.

Trombone: A wind instrument consisting of a cylindrical brass tube which is bent back on itself twice. The central section is so made that the outer tube can slide over the inner, lengthening or shortening the tube and thus giving differences of pitch. The tone is produced by the vibration of the player's lips against the cupped mouthpiece, and is majestic in quality.

Trumpet: A wind instrument having a cylindrical brass tube, a conical bell, and three valves. The tone is produced by the vibration of the player's lips inside the cup-shaped mouthpiece. The range is over two octaves, and the tone is very brilliant and penetrating.

Tuba: The largest instrument of the brass choir. It has a conical brass tube, gradually widening from the mouthpiece to the bell, and usually has four valves. It is the bass of the brass section and has a full, deep tone.

Valse (vals): The French word for "waltz."

Viol: The ancestor of the violin of today. The family of viols were stringed instruments played with a bow, and were in use centuries ago.

Viola: An instrument exactly similar to the violin, but somewhat larger in size and pitched a fifth lower. The strings are heavier than those of the violin and the tone is more somber. It is sometimes called the alto or tenor violin.

Violin: An instrument with four strings tuned in fifths, and played with a bow. In the hands of a skilled performer the tone is extremely beautiful. The violin ranks next to the human voice in flexibility, and has a greater range. It is often called the king of instruments.

Violoncello: From two Italian words meaning "small double bass." It is usually spoken of as the "cello." It has four strings tuned in fifths and played with a bow, and the tone is richer and deeper than that of the violin.

Virtuoso: A public performer, usually an instrumentalist, who has unusual skill.

Vivace (vē-vä'chā): "Vivaciously"; "in a sprightly manner."

Vivo (vē'vō): "Briskly," "rapidly," "animatedly."

Waltz: A graceful salon dance in 3/4 rhythm.

Woodwind: Applied to wind instruments originally made of wood, notably the flute, oboe, clarinet, and bassoon. Some of these, such as the flute and sometimes the clarinet, are now made of metal, but are still referred to as woodwind instruments.

Xylophone: A very old and widely used instrument consisting of strips of wood, graduated in length and resting horizontally. It has a range of two octaves or more and is played with small hammers or mallets.

PRINTED IN THE UNITED STATES OF AMERICA